8/1

.F. de Paula at the airport
ly but leads to same program.
ants to go to Ketchum to
and Antonio on these
wired to cook — B that is not
unless she present ×
hope kind and affectionate
way of judging what that is
in was clearly told, as I lean
could pen. He got pen my own
brackets + But all kind and
in arranging of Alfred's tax
caught that was all this years
mentioned tax

# HEMINGWAY
# IN LOVE

## Also By A. E. Hotchner

# HEMINGWAY

# IN LOVE

## HIS OWN STORY

*A Memoir by*

# A. E. Hotchner

St. Martin's Press
New York

www.stmartins.com

The Library of Congress Cataloging-in-Publication Data is available upon request.

ISBN 978-1-250-07748-6 (hardcover)
ISBN 978-1-4668-8948-4 (e-book)

Our books may be purchased in bulk for promotional, educational,
or business use. Please contact your local bookseller or the
Macmillan Corporate and Premium Sales Department at (800) 221-7945,
extension 5442, or by e-mail at MacmillanSpecialMarkets@macmillan.com.

First Edition: October 2015

10  9  8  7  6  5  4

FOR MY WIFE

*Pamplona, Spain, 1954: Ernest and Hotchner at El Choko bar during La Feria de San Fermín.*

# Contents

*All things truly wicked start from an innocence.*

—ERNEST HEMINGWAY

# Preface

Fifty years ago, a few years after Ernest Hemingway's death, I wrote *Papa Hemingway*, an account of our thirteen years of adventures and misadventures. For those who may not have read it in *Papa*, I am again referring to the spring of 1948, when I was dispatched to Havana on the ridiculous mission of asking Hemingway to write an article on "The Future of Literature." I was with the magazine *Cosmopolitan*, then a literary magazine, before its defoliation by Helen Gurley Brown, and the editor was planning an issue on the future of everything: Frank Lloyd Wright on architecture, Henry Ford II on automobiles, Picasso on art, and, as I said, Hemingway on literature.

Of course, no writer knows the future of literature

beyond what he'll write the next morning, if that, but there I was, checking into the Hotel Nacional for the express purpose of knocking on Hemingway's door and asking him to read his literary tea leaves for good old *Cosmo.* I had tried to avoid this obnoxious assignment, but I was on a "go do it or else" basis, and I could not afford an "or else" as I had been but six months on the job, the only one I had been able to land after dissipating my air force severance pay with a frivolous year in Paris.

As a compromise I took the coward's way out and wrote Hemingway a note, asking him to please send me a brief refusal, which would be very helpful to The Future of Hotchner.

Instead of a note, I received a phone call the next morning from Hemingway, who proposed five o'clock drinks at his favorite Havana bar, the Floridita. He arrived precisely on time, an overpowering presence, not in height, for he was only an inch or so over six feet, but in impact. Everyone in the place responded to his entrance.

The two frozen daiquiris the barman placed in front of us were in conical glasses big enough to hold longstemmed roses.

"Papa Doblas," Ernest said, "the ultimate achievement of the daiquiri maker's art." He conversed with insight and rough humor about famous writers, the Brooklyn

Dodgers, who were there for spring training, actors, prize-fighters, Hollywood phonies, fish, politicians, everything but "The Future of Literature." He left abruptly after our fourth or fifth daiquiri—I lost count—but I was able to retain in the rum mist of my head that he was going to pick me up at six o'clock the next morning and take me on a tour around the Morro Castle waters in his boat, the *Pilar*. When I got back to the hotel, despite the unsteadiness of my pen, I was able to make some notes of our conversation on a sheet of the hotel's stationery. For all the time I knew him, I made a habit of scribbling entries about what had been said and done on any given day. Later on, I augmented these notes with conversations recorded on my Midgetape, a minuscule device the size of my hand, whose tapes allowed ninety minutes of recording time. Ernest and I sometimes corresponded by using them. Although the tapes disintegrated soon after use, I found them helpful.

Steering from topside controls, Ernest took the *Pilar* several hours up the coast. On the way back, we hooked what he referred to as a "stunted marlin," but to me it looked like an unstunted whale. He strapped me into the catch chair and handed me the big heavy rod and reel that had the marlin on the other end. I had never caught anything bigger than a ten-pound bass out of a rowboat and I probably would have had a tough struggle, perhaps even losing the marlin, but Ernest guided me every step of the way, from when to pull up to set the hook to when to bring him in to be taken. The thrill of having reeled in this monster was muted, however, when Ernest and his mate, Gregorio Fuentes, unhooked the marlin and set him free.

"We just might have a new *syndicat des pecheurs*," he said jokingly, "Hotchner and Hemingway, Marlin Purveyors." That took the sting out of not having my picture taken on the dock with the marlin, stunted or not, hanging by its tail beside me.

Over the ensuing years, I would observe Ernest's gentle patience with young people like myself innumerable times. He interacted with them easily. In my case, for example, although I had had military training in firearms, I was a flop at wing shooting, but Ernest patiently led me to proficiency in jump-shooting mallards soaring from canals at the base of the Sawtooth Mountains in Idaho, and cock pheasants breaking from the cornfields. The more our friendship grew, the more I realized that the stories that had circulated about his gruff, pugnacious personality were a myth invented by people who didn't know him but judged him by the subjects he wrote about. He would stand up to any transgressor, yes, but I never saw him as the aggressor.

When we returned from the boat to the Nacional and were saying good-bye in front of the hotel, Ernest said, mentioning it for the first time, "The fact is, I do not know a damn thing about the future of anything."

I assured him it was a dumb request.

He asked what they were paying, and when I said ten thousand dollars, he said well, that was enough to perk up The Future of Something, perhaps a short story, and that we should stay in touch.

We did for the next eight months, culminating in his informing me that he was at work on a novel, which I eventually edited for the magazine. In the process, I accompanied Ernest and his wife, Mary, to Paris and Venice to corroborate the details of certain sections of the novel, *Across the River and into the Trees,* and that was the beginning of our friendship, which over the years took us adventuring to his favorite haunts: hunting for pheasant, wild duck, and Hungarian partridge in Ketchum; bullfighting in Madrid, Málaga, Zaragoza, and the mano a mano competitions of the great matadors Antonio Ordóñez and Luis Miguel Dominguín; deep-sea fishing for marlin; jai alai matches in Havana; the

Auteuil steeplechases in Paris; the World Series and championship prizefights in New York, to name a few.

But looking back on those years, there was one event that seriously interrupted our adventuring: the consecutive plane crashes that Ernest suffered in the African jungle. He had been subjected to a near-death experience in the second of those crashes; that experience upended him, and he was determined to tell me about a painful period in his life that he had never discussed but that he wanted me to know about in case he never got around to telling about it.

Over the following years, while we traveled, he relived the agony of that period in Paris when he was writing *The Sun Also Rises* and at the same time enduring the harrowing experience of being in love with two women simultaneously, an experience that would haunt him to his grave.

Some of these intimate revelations were contained in my original *Papa Hemingway* manuscript, but when, before publication, the publisher, Random House, submitted the script pro forma to their lawyers for vetting, the lawyers put the script through their cautious legal wringer, and as a result, those people involved who were still living had to be stricken. In questioning me about the people depicted, the lawyers even went so far as to require proof that F. Scott Fitzgerald, twenty years dead, was indeed gone.

I also had a personal reason for agreeing to withhold Ernest's reflections at that time. Mary Hemingway was a good, devoted friend, and I felt that learning what Ernest had to say about his first two wives might hurt her feelings, and so would be best kept from her.

These passing years have filtered away all those who were involved during that period. I retained the excised portions of my *Papa* manuscript and have now added considerably more from my original notes, plus material I gleaned back then from my Midgetapes before they disintegrated. And I still have a strong recall of what occurred and what was said during that fateful time in my life.

I can still hear Ernest's distinct manner of speech. He kept no journals or notes, but his retention of conversation was phenomenal. Not only could he conjure up long past exchanges but he could mimic the cadence and style of his contemporaries, such as F. Scott Fitzgerald, Josephine Baker, Gertrude Stein, and other Paris regulars. This incredible ability is exhibited in the dialogue in his novels and short stories. I can personally attest to this skill, since in *The Dangerous Summer* he perfectly re-created a conversation with me, written long after the bullfight event at which the conversation took place.

I once asked him if he kept journals or notes of any kind to supplement his memory. He said, "No, always made things stick. Never kept notes or a journal. Just push the recall button and there it is. If it isn't there, it wasn't worth keeping."

I should add a couple of caveats to that observation. The "recall button" that Ernest pushed to release what he told me during our trips, about a sensitive period in his life, are set forth as relayed to me, with no attempt on my part to correct or alter anything in his recall of people and events of the distant past; although in some instances Ernest may have romanticized or exaggerated or misplaced some things, I regarded these incidental blemishes as part and parcel of who he was. For example, when Ernest referred to Murphy's studio, where he lived after his separation from Hadley, he said it was on the sixth floor. Others who knew Murphy have put the studio on the fifth floor, but in such instances, Ernest's recollections prevail.

My other caveat is that I am by no means a dispassionate participant in the telling of Ernest's story. Over the years, those times Ernest and I were together were no ordinary times for me. He was indeed Papa. I was always aware of his importance, the importance of what he said and did. While my itinerant notes, based on tapes that have long since disintegrated, have aided and abetted my recollections, I have largely relied on my own recall and my own filter in writing this book.

I have lived with Ernest's personal story for a long time. This is not buried memory dredged up. The story he recounted over the course of our travels was entrusted to me with a purpose. I have held that story in trust for these many years, and now I feel it is my fiduciary obligation to Ernest to finally release it from my memory.

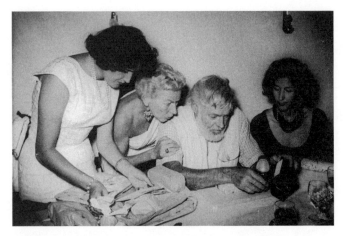

*Churriana, Spain, 1959: Ernest and his wife, Mary, huddled over his presents at his sixtieth birthday party.*

PART ONE

# A Room at
# St. Mary's Hospital

In the beginning of June 1961, on my way back to New York from Hollywood, I took a flight that stopped in Minneapolis. From there, I rented a car and drove ninety miles to St. Mary's Hospital in Rochester. For the second time, my close friend—Ernest Hemingway—was a patient in its psychiatric section, under the care of doctors from the nearby Mayo Clinic. I had previously visited him there during his first confinement, on my way to Hollywood several weeks earlier.

For the past six weeks, Ernest had not been allowed to make or receive phone calls or to have visitors, not even his wife, Mary, while he was undergoing a series of ECT (electroconvulsive therapy) treatments. Now, during a respite before continuing with another series of ECTs, his Mayo Clinic doctors permitted him to phone me and arrange for a visit.

The Mayo Clinic itself had no hospital facilities; an affiliation existed, however, with Rochester's St. Mary's Hospital, run by an energetic order of nuns, who allowed the clinic's doctors to treat patients they hospitalized there.

Back then, electric shock was brutally administered, the electric current projected into the patient's brain without benefit of an anesthetic, a piece of wood clenched between his teeth as he writhed in torturous pain. The Mayo doctors had diagnosed Ernest as suffering from a depressive persecutory condition and had prescribed the ECTs in an attempt to diminish it.

There had been many conjectural explanations at the time for his downturn: that he had terminal cancer or money problems; that he had quarreled with Mary. None was true. As his intimate friends knew, he had been suffering from depression and paranoia for the past year of his life, but the roots of this suffering had not been uncovered, if, indeed, they ever would be. I had tried to reason with him, attempting to help him overcome some of his destructive phobias, but the little progress we made turned out to be deceptively temporary. I had also tried to get him away from his destructive environment by arranging an extensive tour of all those fishing places around the world he had always coveted, but on the eve of departure, he backed off. And when Mary urged him to see a psychiatrist, he said hell no, he already had a psychiatrist, his Corona typewriter.

Ernest and I saw each other often during the thirteen years of our friendship. I dramatized many of his stories and novels for television specials, theater, and movies. We shared adventures in France, Italy, Cuba, Mexico, and Spain. The summer before the onset of his delusions, Ernest and I had enjoyed a glorious bull-fighting tour of the many cities in Spain where the mano a mano competitions between Spain's reigning matadors—the brothers-in-law Antonio Ordóñez and Luis Miguel Dominguín—were staged (the deadly mano a mano combat between two competing matadors instead of the usual three). In one of those cities, Cuidad Real, Antonio dressed me in one of his matador get-ups, assigned "El Pecas" (The Freckled One) as my name, and Ernest induced me to go into the bullring as *sobre-saliente* (a third matador who fights the bull only if the two matadors on the bill are gored and disabled) for these great matadors, while he posed as my manager. As *sobre-saliente,* I had to make one obligatory pass for the crowd, but Ernest told me to stick close to Antonio, who helped me bring it off by imperceptibly enticing the bull to charge him.

Ernest's zest for life was infectious.

In July of 1959, we had celebrated Ernest's sixtieth birthday in Churriana, a village in the hills above Málaga, with a wonderful party that lasted two days. Mary Hemingway, who was Ernest's fourth wife, pulled out all the stops on this one. She felt that Ernest's previous birthdays, because of his lack of cooperation, had always been observed with a pause rather than a celebration, and she was determined to make up for all the lost parties with this one. She succeeded.

There was champagne from Paris, Chinese food from London, *bacalao à la Vizcaína* (a Basque-style codfish stew) from Madrid, a shooting booth from a traveling carnival, a fireworks expert from Valencia (the citadel of fireworks), flamenco dancers from Málaga, and musicians from Torremolinos. Celebrants came from all over and included the Maharajah of Jaipur with his maharani and son; the Maharajah of Cooch Behar with his maharani; Gen. C. P. "Buck" Lanham from Washington, D.C. (he commanded the troops in the Hürtgen Forest battle, which Ernest joined ex officio, in World War II); Ambassador and Mrs. David Bruce, who flew down from Bonn; various Madrid notables; and many of Ernest's old Paris pals.

Ernest thoroughly enjoyed himself. At the shooting booth, he used a decrepit old rifle to shoot cigarette butts from the lips of both the Maharajah of Cooch Behar and Antonio Ordóñez, Spain's numero uno matador. He led a conga line around the grounds and delighted in opening his mound of presents and holding them up for all to see.

The highlight of the party occurred when the firecracker wizard from Valencia fired a salvo of giant rockets, which landed in the top of a royal palm tree near the house and set the treetop on fire. The Málaga fire department was alerted, and the hook and ladder that arrived was straight out of a Mack Sennett comedy, as were the firemen. They scaled the tree and extinguished the blaze, and then Ernest immediately assimilated them into the party. For the rest of the night, Ernest wore the fire chief's metal hat; Antonio appropriated the fire engine and raced around the grounds, with Ernest beside him and the siren blaring.

The end of that summer was the last of the good times.

Over the following year, I witnessed rather abrupt and puzzling changes in Ernest's demeanor: his tortured inability to condense *The Dangerous Summer* for *Life* magazine; for the first time since he lived there, not participating in the annual pheasant shoot near his home in Ketchum, Idaho; his sudden insistence that fields he had always hunted were now off-limits. As his paranoia deepened, he became convinced that his car and house were being bugged by the FBI and that IRS agents were auditing his bank account.

On my last visit to Ketchum, Mary, Ernest, and I went to dinner the night before I left. Halfway through the meal, Ernest, who seemed to be enjoying himself, suddenly grew tense and whispered that we had to leave the restaurant immediately. Mary asked what was wrong.

"Those two FBI agents at the bar, that's what's wrong."

Later that night, Mary pulled me aside. She was terribly distraught. Ernest spent hours every day with the manuscript of his Paris pieces, trying to write but unable to do more than turn its pages. He often spoke of destroying himself and would sometimes stand at the gun rack holding one of his guns and staring out the window. After much prodding, his Ketchum doctor induced him to enter, under an assumed name, the psychiatric section of St. Mary's, where his Mayo doctors performed a series of ECTs.

He called me from the hall phone outside his room.

He sounded in control, but his voice held a forced heartiness that didn't belong there. His delusions had not changed or diminished: His room was bugged; his phone was tapped; he suspected that one of the interns was a fed. I had hoped his treatment would make him less fixated on his catalog of injustices, but, unfortunately, the phone call demonstrated that, if anything, they had intensified.

After he had undergone the series of ECTs, along with many sessions with the psychiatrists, I visited him for the first time, on my way out to Hollywood, again hoping he would be less pursued by his delusions; but, no, the same obsessions haunted him.

Inconceivably, Ernest was released by the Mayo doctors soon after my visit. He called me in Hollywood to say how delighted he was to be home in Ketchum and back at work. He had gone hunting the day after his return, he said, and there were eight mallards and two teals now hanging over the woodpile outside the kitchen window.

His bonhomie was short-lived, however. His old trepidations soon found their way back and, in fact, intensified. He twice attempted suicide with a gun from his vestibule rack and was stopped only by vigorous physical intervention. During a return flight to St. Mary's, though heavily sedated, he struggled to jump from the plane. When it stopped in Caspar, Wyoming, for repairs, he tried to walk into a moving propeller.

As I reached the outskirts of Rochester in my rented Chevy on that June day in 1961, I was feeling anxious about Ernest's condition. I hoped the latest round of ECTs, along with accelerated sessions with the Mayo psychiatrists, had eliminated Ernest's phobias, or at least reduced their hold on him.

I checked into my hotel and went directly to the hospital. The head nurse opened Ernest's door for me with her key, a foreboding. The room was small, but it had a large window that admitted abundant sunshine. There were no flowers and the walls were bare. On a table beside the bed were three stacked books, and next to the table was a straight-backed metal chair. There were metal bars horizontally across the window.

Ernest was facing the window, his back to the door, standing at a hospital table that had been raised to serve him as a desk. He was wearing his old red woolen bathrobe (christened by Mary the "Emperor's Robe"), which was secured with a worn leather belt that had a large buckle embossed *"Gott Mit Uns,"* a belt he had liberated from a dead German soldier during World War II's battle of Hürtgen Forest. He wore his favorite scuffed Indian moccasins and a soiled white tennis visor over his eyes. His beard was scraggly and he seemed to have lost quite a bit of weight.

"Mr. Hemingway, your guest is here," the nurse said.

Ernest turned; the startled look on his face held for a moment and then faded into a broad smile as he connected with me. He came to greet me, pulling off his visor as we wrapped our arms around each other Spanish-style and thumped each other's backs. He was genuinely glad I had come. He appeared attenuated, as if the man he once was had disappeared and the man before me was only a marker to show who he had been.

"Well, Hotch," he said, "welcome to Never Never Land, where they frisk you and lock the door on you and don't have the decency to trust you with a blunt instrument."

The nurse was standing in the doorway.

"Nurse Susan," Ernest said, introducing me, "this is El Pecas, the famous matador. Pecas, this is Susan who holds the key to my heart."

That got a laugh out of both of us.

I gave her a tin of caviar I had brought for Ernest, to keep in the refrigerator.

Ernest and I sat for a while, he on the bed, me on the chair, and at first he sounded like he was back on solid ground, but to my dismay, he began to lapse into a repetition of his old miseries: the room was bugged, also the telephone outside the door; poverty complaints; accusations against his banker, his lawyer, his doctor in Ketchum, all the fiduciary people in his life; worries about not having proper clothes; distraught over imagined taxes. There was much repetition.

I stood up, intent on directing him away from the same grievances that had assailed him when I had visited him during his previous confinement. The ECTs obviously hadn't affected them. I walked over to the table and asked him what he was working on.

"Paris."

He was referring to his impressions of Paris and of some of the people he knew when he first went to live there with his first wife, Hadley, back in the early twenties.

"How's it going?"

"That's the worst of it. I can't finish the book. I *can't.* I've been at this damn table day after day after day after day. All I need is . . . maybe a sentence, maybe more, I don't know, and I can't get it. Not any of it, you understand? I've written Scribner to scratch the book. It was all set for the fall, but I had to scratch it."

I asked him if these were the sketches from the Ritz trunk, the ones I had read.

He said they were, plus a final new one, which mattered most.

"But those sketches," I said, "as wonderful about Paris as anyone can hope to write."

On one of our trips to Paris, when we were staying at the Ritz (the time our Hemhotch syndicate won a steeplechase race at Auteuil that paid 27–1), we had lunch one day with Charles Ritz, who had succeeded his father, César. Charles informed Ernest that in redoing the hotel's storage area, they had recently discovered a Louis Vuitton trunk that Ernest had stored there in the thirties. It was a trunk that Vuitton himself had made for Ernest, and he was delighted to see it come back to him. We opened it in Charles's office, and among other things inside, there were a number of schoolboy blue notebooks in which Ernest had written about Paris in the twenties and the people he knew during his early years there. Ernest had given me the sketches to read; they were exquisite, poetic, penetrating, callous, timeless, like no one had ever written about Paris and the fascinating people of the twenties who were Ernest's contemporaries.

There was a rap on the door and nurse Susan came in. She said that Ernest's doctor wanted him for some tests but that he wouldn't be long. Ernest took a sheaf of papers from his improvised desk and handed them to me to read until he came back. He said this was a chapter I hadn't read, the one that would conclude the book, the one that had to count.

I pulled the chair over to the window and began to read the handwritten sketch that Ernest had left with me. Entitled "There Is Never Any End to Paris," it was different from the other sketches I had read that time at the Ritz, sketches that concentrated on Paris neighborhoods and the people Ernest had known back then: Gertrude Stein, Sylvia Beach (an American-born bookseller and publisher), Ford Madox Ford, Ezra Pound, Scott Fitzgerald among them. This sketch I was now reading was obviously intended to be the book's finale; what made it different was that this one was written both as a tribute to his struggling but wonderful early years in Paris and as a lament for how it turned out for him, and what had caused it.

Overall, it was a fervid declaration of love directed toward his first wife, Hadley, the memory of her in their fourth-floor walk-up on Rue Cardinal-Lemoine, and then where they had lived with their infant son, Bumby, at 113 Rue Notre-Dame-des-Champs, on the second floor, above a sawmill in the courtyard, and how, wrapped in sweaters, Hadley had played on an old piano Ernest had rented for her in the frigid basement of the local patisserie.

In the sketch, Ernest also reveled in his skiing adventures with Hadley: Schruns in the Voralberg in Austria, where they both learned to ski and where the rooms at the Taube Inn had big windows, big beds with good blankets and feather coverlets, and served splendid breakfasts with big cups of coffee, fresh bread and fruit preserves, eggs, and good ham; the Madlenerhaus, the beautiful old inn where they slept close together in a big bed under a feather quilt, the window open and the stars close.

Halfway through the sketch, however, Ernest veered off the romantic early years with Hadley, when they were very poor but happy, to describe what happened to their idyllic life when the rich people appeared, led by a pilot fish, neither the rich nor the pilot fish identified. When there are two people who love each other, Ernest wrote, the rich are attracted to them but that he and Hadley were naifs who did not know how to protect themselves. Charmed by these rich, Ernest admitted he was as stupid as a bird dog who goes out with anyone with a gun.

And, most important, there was another of the rich, an unmarried woman who coveted Ernest and befriended Hadley as a means of infiltrating their lives and breaking up their marriage. Ernest confessed that he had been seduced by the simultaneous attention of these two women and that he had the bad luck of being in love with both of them.

Before he ended his life, it was important to him that his final words explain the self-inflicted pain of letting the only true love of his life slip away. The tragedy of having loved two women at the same time had bedeviled him all his life. It was after he had a near-death experience in a plane crash that he decided to relive those perilous days that had consumed him back in the twenties, when he initially went to Paris, diluting the pleasure of the publication of his first novel, *The Sun Also Rises*. Ernest relived those years by describing them to me, and in the telling he found some measure of closure. But over the years of his life, it was an irreparable tragedy, one that he was never able to overcome, not through fame or plaudits or the profits of genius.

I had read the chapter twice and let it settle in while Ernest was meeting with his doctor. In his summing up of his Paris years—the people, the places, the reversals, the triumphs, the fulfillments, the disappointments, the redolent recollections of life with Hadley—I was surprised he had omitted so many telltale revelations, like the one-hundred-day suspension of his marriage, which he had once told me about. It may be that his persecuted mind and his dire struggle to write precluded a full accounting, or perhaps he had intended that I be the custodian of his account of the tragic fallout of loving two women at the same time, the debacle from which he never extricated himself.

There was a rap on the door and nurse Susan came in to tell me the blood pressure tests were going to be a while longer and that if I preferred to wait in the lounge, where it was more comfortable, she'd come to get me. I told her I'd rather wait where I was.

So sitting there at the window with the final chapter in my lap, I began to think about the plane crash—in fact, the two crashes—that led me to meet up with Ernest at the Gritti Palace Hotel in Venice in 1954.

*Uganda, Africa, 1954: Wreckage of the first of Ernest's two consecutive plane crashes.*

PART TWO

# Rendezvous at the Gritti Palace Hotel in Venice

It was on the morning of January 25, 1954, that word flashed around the world that Ernest Hemingway and his wife, Mary, had been killed in a plane crash in dense jungle near Murchison Falls in Uganda, setting off universal mourning and obituaries. But news of the tragedy was soon superseded by a report that Ernest had suddenly, miraculously, emerged from the jungle at Butiabe carrying a bunch of bananas and a bottle of Gordon's gin. To the startled reporters who rushed to interview him, Ernest announced, according to an AP dispatch, "My luck, she is running good."

A few hours later, however, his luck ran not so good. A rescue plane, a de Havilland Rapide, a 1930s-era biplane fashioned out of plywood, was sent to the crash site to fly

Ernest and Mary back to their base in Kenya, but the de Havilland crashed on takeoff and burst into flames; it was that second crash that left its mark on Ernest.

I sent numerous cables trying to reach him and eventually received a return cable asking me to phone him at the Gritti Palace Hotel in Venice. At that moment, I was in the Hague on assignment for a magazine, interviewing Queen Beatrice and her resident fortune-teller whom the queen consulted for royal guidance.

I phoned Ernest and he urged me to conclude my royal interrogatory and come to the Gritti. He said, "I have a new Lancia with a good professional driver to take us over the Alps and along the Corniche to Pamplona for the Feria of San Fermín. Would like your company on the trip. I'm beat up from those kites falling all over Africa."

In the past he had called me often about pleasurable trips to desirable destinations, but this was the first time it was for a personal situation. He sounded self-conscious.

When I got to his corner room at the Gritti, Ernest was sitting in a chair by the window, tennis visor in place, reading his worldwide obituaries from a stack of newspapers on the desk beside him. I stood for a moment in the open doorway, shocked at his appearance. I had last seen him in New York in the fall of 1953, shortly before he had left for Africa. What was shocking to me now was how he had aged in the intervening five months. What there was of his hair (most of it had been burned off) had turned from brindle to white, as had his singed beard, and he appeared to have diminished somewhat; I don't mean physically diminished, but some of the aura of indomitableness seemed to have gone out of him.

Suddenly, he blurted aloud from the obit he was reading: "'Swashbuckling ruffian of literature!'" and a laugh roared out of him. He picked up his wineglass from the table beside him and drained its contents.

That's when he saw me, and a wide smile spread across his face as he motioned for me to help him emerge from the depths of his chair. "I feel like a creature coming up from the deep," he said as I helped pull him upright.

"How are you, Papa?" I asked. "I mean the true gen," using a favorite expression of his that referred to distinguishing between fact and innuendo.

"Right arm and shoulder dislocated," he said, "ruptured kidney, back gone to hell, face, belly, hand, especially hand, all charred by the de Havilland fire. Lungs scalded by smoke. Come on, I'll show you the evidence in Technicolor."

He led me into the bathroom. On a table in the corner between the tub and the sink were half a dozen glasses containing urine. Ernest picked up one of them and exhibited its dark contents in the light. He said, "Couldn't piss for two days on account of plugged somewhere with kidney-cell stuff. Look at it—floating around like quill toothpicks. Color spooks me. Prune juice. Doctor on boat coming here from Africa very good. Gave me stuff for kidneys, scissored away all dead flesh from the burns—very classy doctor, said I should have died at the crash. Said I still might. Put me on a strict diet. Tell you the truth, I was really spooked you had lost a member of our firm when the de Havilland crashed and crumbled and burst into flames. I was in the rear section, Mary up front with the pilot, Roy Marsh. They got out all right, but the fire was broiling the rear metal door, which was bent and smashed. I was choking from the smoke; besides, there was no room to get to the jammed door to push on it. That second, right there, I felt I was checking out. I've had bum raps before—ramming that water tower in blackout London, which leveled me and blasted my head open; the car wrecks in Idaho that broke bone, the direct hit in the trench in Fossalta, some others—but I always felt I'd make it and the hell with the grim son of a bitch with his scythe, but this time, frying in that sardine can, busted all over, I thought, Shitmaru, it's the finish line, they've nailed me to the cross and lit the fire, but somehow I cleared enough space to reach the door that was bent and jammed and with my good left shoulder and my head I was able to force it open enough to squeeze out.

"We stood there, helplessly watching the de Havilland burn up. My clothes were smoking. I made several scientific notations that might interest students of the alcoholic occult. First noted were four little pops, which I chalked up as belonging to our four bottles of Carlsberg beer. Then there was a more substantial pop, which I credited to the bottle of Grand Macnish. But the only really good bang came from the Gordon's gin. It was an unopened bottle with a metal top. The Grand Macnish was corked and, besides, was half gone, but the Gordon's had real éclat."

He went back to his chair and poured two glasses of champagne from a bottle in a silver ice bucket on an end table. He said reading all his obituaries had made him feel better but that now that he had leveled with me about how beat-up he was . . . he'd always held back on the stuff he was going to write, inventory, insurance against the dry-up . . . but the way he was feeling now, he thought they'd shortened him out, and he would tell me some of it so if he never actually got around to it, then someone would know. "Like the one hundred days. You know about the hundred days?"

I said I didn't.

"I don't mean to sound like a morbid, but every time you take out insurance, it's an act of morbidity, isn't it? You still keep your notes?"

I said I did, and the Midgetapes.

"And I have mine. We're in good shape."

Ernest had reserved a dinner table in the Gritti's historic dining room, but he said he felt too rocky for public dining, so he opted for the room-service menu. It was a large room with high, arching windows facing the Grand Canal, beautifully furnished with Venetian antique furniture, so being served in front of those windows, with gondolas floating below, was certainly not an imposition.

Ernest ordered calves liver (*fegato alla Veneziana*), which he said was a restorative, and he ordered a bottle of Valpolicella Superiore, which he told the floor waiter to pour for us without waiting for the bottle to breathe. "Italian reds don't need oxygen," he said. "I got that bit of Bacchanalian wisdom from Fitzgerald."

I said, "You got a lot from Fitzgerald, didn't you?"

"Got and gave," Ernest said. "Met him first in Paris at the Dingo Bar. Introduced himself. Of course I knew who he was. His short stories in *The Saturday Evening Post*, one of them, 'The Diamond as Big as the Ritz,' hell of a story.

Scott loved the Ritz, had a regular spot in the main bar-room. Sometimes he'd invite me for a drink and I'd have to spruce up my old corduroy jacket with my one necktie, which was so corkscrewed, it could have opened bottles. Scott didn't fraternize with other writers living in Paris, like Ezra Pound, Dos Passos, Archibald MacLeish, but he sort of took me on as my sponsor and mentor. Scott was going on thirty, which he thought was the end of his road, and I think he viewed me as a possible redemption project, but I didn't know why, because he had made a solid name for himself with *The Beautiful and Damned* and *The Great Gatsby*, which had just been published. He asked to see some of my short stories, even though they'd been roundly rejected.

"I felt self-conscious giving them to someone as fa-mous as he was, but after reading them, he said that one of them, 'Fifty Grand,' was damned good but would be better if I shucked the first page and started on page two, that the story had more muscle that way. I thought about that and agreed that to start the story, less would be better. Scott said he would send it to his editor, Max Perkins at Scribner if it was okay with me. He had written to him about me and said he'd like him to see my work. Scott had a copy of his new book for me, *The Great Gatsby,* hoped I would like it.

"I thought it was one of the best books in a long time,

in fact I told him that. Although he had attained considerable fame and I had yet to prove myself, there was a sense of bonding from the very beginning, a sense of brotherhood, a right to intrude on each other's lives, as if we were somehow responsible for the other one's missteps and misdemeanors.

"Max Perkins did like 'Fifty Grand' and helped getting it published in *The Atlantic Monthly*, with a princely payment of three hundred and fifty dollars, which provided winter shoes for Hadley and regular trips to the *boucherie*.

"Scott wanted us to meet Zelda and invited us to lunch at their apartment on Rue de Tilsitt, a dark, lifeless place. Hadley and I were put off by Zelda, who seemed intent on stuffing her non sequiturs into the conversation. She spoke about how much time Scott devoted to writing, more with resentment than support, jealous of his writing pad, as if it were a seductive mistress.

"Scott introduced me to some of his group, the ones who shared his boozy adventures. One of those favorites was Lady Duff Twysden, a character right out of a very good English novel who had lost her way. Her look was original, her chic was original, and God knows her speech and her capacity for drink were all original. She wore a man's hat tilted over her sculptured blond hair and mannish tweeds that somehow made her look seductive. She was separated from Sir Roger Thomas Twysden, tenth baronet, and, according to her, a sadistic martinet. Humiliated her wherever they went, denigrated her looks, family, intelligence, education. Said he didn't know why he'd married her. And yet doesn't want a divorce. Drinks himself purple on his huge estate, gives lavish parties, different women as hostesses, claims not to know where she is or if she is. 'I don't give a damn,' Duff said, since she got a monthly stipend, although not quite enough to get from one month to the next. The humiliation hurts, but Harold and Pat adore her—she needs that, she said, and they contribute to her shortfall."

I asked Ernest about Harold and Pat and he explained that Harold Loeb was Princeton from a very rich New York family, had been on the boxing and wrestling teams in college. He had literary aspirations, even started a little magazine in Paris called *Broom.* Fiercely devoted to Duff, very jealous of Pat, who alternated weekends with Duff.

Pat Guthrie, Duff's distant cousin, Ernest said, was a waspish Scot who appeared to be in a rather perpetual state of inebriation; he regularly gave Duff money from his allowance.

Ernest said that the three of them were inseparable despite the fact that Pat and Harold were constantly at each other. "They often invited me to join them when I finished writing. I'd write mornings either on a table in the Closerie des Lilas, a good café near our apartment, or in a little room I had rented, sixth-floor walk-up in an old hotel, and then find them at the Select, their favorite hangout. The Fitzgeralds sometimes invited the three of them and us to dinner, and on one occasion two sisters, Pauline and Ginny Pfeiffer."

"So that's how you met Pauline? What was your take on her?"

"First impression? Small, flat-chested, not nearly as attractive as her sister. Pauline had recently come to Paris to work at *Vogue* magazine, and she looked like she'd just stepped out of its pages. Up-to-date fashion. Close-cropped hair like a boy's, à la mode back then, short, fringed dress, loops of pearls, costume jewelry, rouged, bright red lips. Said she had attended the Visitation Convent in St. Louis, a few blocks from where Hadley had lived.

"I never gave Pauline another thought after that dinner. Hadley was the only woman who mattered in my life, her full body and full breasts, hair long to her shoulders, long-sleeved dresses at her ankles, little or no jewelry or makeup. I adored her looks and the feel of her in bed, and that's how it was. She lived her life loving the things I loved: skiing in Austria, picnics on the infield at the Auteuil races, staying up all night at the bicycle races at the Vélodrome, fortified with sandwiches and a thermos of coffee, trips to alpine villages to watch the Tour de France, fishing in the Irati, the bullfights in Madrid and Pamplona, hiking in the Black Forest.

"Even though I never thought about Pauline after that first encounter, as I was to find out, she had serious thoughts about me, thoughts that became schemes and ruses, subterfuges, connivances."

"How did she get into your life?" I asked.

"I think it began," Ernest said, "with a conversation that Pauline and Ginny had with Hadley that evening at the Fitzgeralds'. Hadley had told them about our son, Bumby, and they asked if they could visit. And they did. Brought him presents from that swank toy store on Rue Saint-Honoré. Pauline took a liking to Hadley, invited her to tea at the Crillon, to some of the fashion showings, brought her fashion magazines and books. Occasionally I'd see Pauline and Ginny in the Dingo when I'd be having a drink with Scott or Dos Passos, and sometimes they joined us. Ginny was much more attractive than Pauline, who was smaller, kind of a boy look. They knew the latest slang and smoked cigarettes from ivory holders. Ginny usually had an affectionate lady friend in tow, so that narrowed the field. I wondered if being a lesbo ran in the family. Didn't matter. The sisters were witty and up-to-the-minute, but I wasn't interested. Life with Hadley was solid.

"Occasionally, they'd come by my workplace end of a day, that little bare room I had rented on the fifth floor, sans heat, sans lift, sans most everything, in the old shabby hotel on Rue Mouffetard. They'd corral me for drinks at a nearby café, bringing good humor and wit and liveliness to what had been a frustrating, unproductive day. After a time, Ginny didn't come anymore and Pauline came alone, looking up-to-the-minute chic, cheerful and exuding admiration, which, of course, after a tough day felt good. She had a genuine or feigned affection for Bumby, visited him, took him to Punch and Judy shows in the Tuileries, offered to babysit whenever Hadley and I wanted to go out, but broke as we were, we never took her up on it, since we didn't have the scratch to go anywhere.

"Pauline would invite us to a restaurant, suggesting that our *femme de ménage*, Marie Cocotte, look after Bumby, but Pauline knew Hadley was loath to leave Bumby at night and she knew Hadley would urge me to go without her. Of course I was broke and Pauline paid whenever I did go. She was clever and entertaining and full of desire. She had the 'I get what I want' hubris of a very rich girl who won't be denied. The Pfeiffer clan owned the town of Piggott, Arkansas. Pauline's old man owned the bank, the cotton gin and the corn, wheat, soybeans, and other stuff produced by his tenant farmers. Also a chain of drugstores and God knows what else—maybe all of Arkansas. Her uncle Gus had all the money her father didn't have—he owned Richard Hudnut perfume, Sloan's liniment, Warner Pharmaceuticals, and other such shit. Gus was childless and he fawned on Pauline—whatever she wanted, all she had to do was ask."

I asked him how he felt being around someone so rich when he was so poor.

He took a while answering. He teased his beard and looked away, as if consulting something in the distance. The scalded patches on his face added years to his looks.

"Back then, to be honest, probably liked it—poverty's a disease that's cured by the medicine of money. I guess I liked the way she spent it—designer clothes, taxis, restaurants. Later on, when reality got to me, I saw the rich for what they were: a goddamn blight like the fungus that kills tomatoes. I set the record straight in 'Snows of Kilimanjaro,' but Harry, who's laid up with a gangrenous leg, is too far gone by then and he dies without forgiving the rich. I think I still feel the way Harry felt about the rich in the story. Always will."

Ernest summoned the floor waiter and discussed wines with him. They decided on an interesting Chianti.

Ernest asked if I had been to the *feria* in Pamplona, the annual bullfight festival that honored their patron saint.

I said I hadn't.

He proceeded to describe a trip there with Lady Duff Twysden and her group, a trip that would be the turning point both in his writing life and his other life. "Pamplona then was its own true self," Ernest said, "before the tourists ruined it. The lure of those ten days with Duff and company goaded me into trying to capture it on paper. I started to write soon after we left Pamplona, and for the next five weeks it overwhelmed me, like I had a fever that roared through my head every day, and left me as empty as the pod of a shelled pea. But by morning I was reloaded and ready to fever my way through another day. That fever was an out-of-control brush fire that swept me into Pauline's maw. She'd have me for a drink in her attractive apartment on Rue Picot, and that started it.

"I first called the book *Fiesta,* only later on *The Sun Also Rises.* Over those five weeks, I wrote it in various places, promising myself that when I returned to Paris, I'd avoid Pauline, but the fever of writing and rewriting opened me up to her. She'd persisted herself into a narcotic, and though I hate to admit it, I became as attached to her as I was to Hadley."

He refilled his wineglass. I passed.

"You ever loved two women at the same time?"

I said I hadn't.

"Lucky boy," he said. "It was complicated, like that time on the Riviera. Our drive to Pamplona will take us over the Alps onto the Grande Corniche and at Antibes— I'll show you the villa where we were staying on Cap d'Antibes, the place Bumby had his whooping cough. Actually, there were two adjoining villas separated by an iron fence with ornamental spikes. The larger villa was the Villa Saint-Louis, where the Murphys and their guests stayed; the small one was the Villa Paquita, where we were. You know about the Murphys?"

I didn't.

He explained that Gerald and Sara Murphy were a very rich young American couple who lived in Paris. They were celebrity collectors, predominantly artists and writers. Ernest said he met them via Fitzgerald. He said of course he wasn't a celebrity (*The Sun Also Rises* hadn't been published yet), but it was the coldest and iciest winter in Paris in God knows how many years and he thought the Murphys took pity on them and invited them to come down to the Riviera. They brought Marie Cocotte, to look after Bumby, who had a nagging cough.

"The Fitzgeralds, John Dos Passos and Archie and Ada MacLeish were guests of the Murphys and we all enjoyed beach time and dinners together. But soon after we arrived, Bumby's cough got worse, and Sara Murphy, concerned about her young children, summoned a doctor, who found that Bumby had whooping cough and that's when all three of us were quarantined. Of course that cut off any contact with the Murphy house but they came every evening at sundown, bringing their drinks and hors d'oeuvres to the spiked fence and we shouted back and forth, us on the veranda. After a while all those spikes were decorated with upside-down booze bottles, Scott's leading the way.

"Pauline had been writing me, sending cables, making sure I kept her in my sights. She was on vacation, staying here at the Danieli with her uncle Gus and aunt Beatrice, when I wrote and told her where we were staying on the Riviera and that we were quarantined with Bumby's whooping cough."

"And?"

"She said she missed me and that since she'd had whooping cough as a child she'd come visit, since she was immune and I could explain she was coming to help with Bumby."

"And you said okay?"

"That's my regret—I didn't tell her not to, a four-legged regret with six sharp horns."

Ernest got up and went to the bathroom. When he returned he settled in his chair and refreshed his wine.

"Soon after the quarantine, Pauline Pfeiffer showed up. I'd already told Hadley she was coming to help out with Bumby. Pauline moved into a room next to ours and right away she took charge. Brought the morning coffee and croissants to our room, sat on the edge of my side of the bed while we three shared our *petit déjeuner*. I was nervous but excited with her there. She went to the beach with us every day, and even though Hadley had a sketchy back from a childhood accident, Pauline insisted on trying to teach her to dive. Poor Hadley wound up with days of back pain. Pauline was just as set on teaching Hadley to play bridge, though Hadley was hopeless. One thing Hadley did enjoy was our long afternoon bike rides all over the streets of Juan-les-Pins.

"When the quarantine was lifted, we spent our evenings at the Murphys'. Pauline stayed on, although Bumby wasn't whooping anymore. And when the Murphys' lease on Villa Paquita ran out, I booked a room at the Hôtel de la Pinède down the beach from us. Pauline took a room right next to ours. Bumby and Marie stayed in a little place next to the hotel.

"Pauline kept expressing her gratitude to Hadley for letting her be with our family. Said it was very difficult being an American women alone in France. Said Hadley was like a sister, but"—Ernest started to laugh—"she never had her *petit déjeuner* on sister Hadley's side of the bed."

I asked Ernest if Hadley had complained to him about Pauline's presence.

"Yes, at times she was a little annoyed but Pauline kept saying that she hoped she wasn't intruding and so forth which made Hadley assure her we were pleased to have her. Looking back on it, I guess I was happy to have two attractive women looking after me, but at the same time I was certainly uncomfortable.

"Occasionally I'd sneak down to a little beach café with Scott to get a break from the group at the Murphys'. The last time we were at this café was when Scott opened up on me. He said he could see it coming right from the start. I knew what he was going to say but I played dumb. 'What do you mean? Start of what?' He said, 'I've got eyes. The way she looks at you. Hangs around. Coddles Hadley. Now showing up here. You are being set up by a femme fatale. When she first arrived in Paris word was out that she was shopping for a husband.'

"I was annoyed having him bring it up, but also eager to talk about it.

" 'She wants you for herself,' he said, 'and she'll do anything to get you.'

"I leveled with him and confessed I loved both of them.

"He said he'd give it to me straight: 'She's going to bust up your marriage if you don't get rid of her.'

"I said I really wanted to, I tried, but damn it, I just couldn't.

"Scott got angry, said I sure as hell could and he'd tell me how. 'Just say, "Pauline, you're a terrific woman, but I'd like you to get the hell out of my life, because if you don't, I'll lose my wife and my little son and my whole existence." Why'd you let yourself get into this mess?'

"Naïve, that's all naïve. A very attractive woman shows up, becomes friendly with Hadley, goes places with both of us, is totally interested in me and my work, free and willing to keep me company, to go places when Hadley is tied down with Bumby—all the signs she's got me in her sights but I don't recognize any of 'em. All I see is after a really tough day writing, there're two women waiting for me, giving me their attention, caring about me, women both appealing, but in different ways. Told Scott I liked having them around. Stimulating, fires me up, and before I know it, I'm in love with both of them, totally naïve, never suspecting Pauline wasn't there as a single woman enjoying being around a family but a woman who wanted to break us up and get me for herself. But now I love them both. May bring me bad luck but hope not. Hope we can go along like this.

"Scott said, step easy, I was walking on eggshells. He quoted an old piece of wisdom: 'A man, torn between two women, will eventually lose 'em both.'

"I said yes I was torn but that I needed both of them and intended to keep them, somehow.

"Scott said I was a sad son of a bitch who didn't know a damn thing about women. He gripped my arm and pulled me toward him. Raised his voice. 'Get rid of her! Now! Right here! It's a three-alarm fire! Now's the time! Tell her!'

"We finished our drinks and walked back to the villa to join the others. That night I thought about talking to Pauline, actually started to but, hell, I couldn't."

"So you never followed Fitzgerald's advice?"

"I wanted to, damn it, but what happened, I'd go off, try to work her out of me, thought I had, but I'd go back to Paris and Pauline'd get it going again. But to allay Hadley's suspicions, Pauline kept up the pretense of caring about her. I truly loved Hadley and I wanted to get us straight again. So I decided to get us out of Paris and the temptation of Pauline. Hadley and I packed up that winter and went to Schruns [an Austrian ski resort] with Bumby to ski. We stayed at the Hotel Taube, a couple of dollars a day for all three of us. I was going to cut

Pauline off. But, shitmaru, she followed us to Schruns, booked herself into the Taube, said she wanted to learn to ski, would I give her lessons. Hadley wasn't happy about it but she was a good sport. Actually, Pauline wasn't nearly as good as Hadley skiing or horseback riding, shooting, fishing, name it.

"When she had to go back to Paris to do the collections for *Vanity Fair,* I was relieved that maybe alone with Hadley I could shape up and lose the pressure of loving both of them.

"But a cable arrived from Max Perkins, editor at Scribner, with the terrific news they were going to publish *Sun Also Rises.* Would I go to New York for contracts and all that. I took off for Paris immediately and booked myself on the first decent boat, four days later. Hadley and Bumby stayed in Schruns and I said I'd return as soon as I got back from New York. I checked into the Hôtel Vénétia in Montparnasse.

"Pauline showed up the minute I stepped foot in Paris. Those four days she clung to me like ivy on a wall, taking me to nightclubs, Michelin restaurants, the Paris Opéra. I spent those four nights in her bed in her attractive apartment on the Rue Picot until my boat left for New York."

Ernest summoned the floor waiter for a bottle of Barolo. He said it had the joy of Italy in it. There was a large cut of Parmesan cheese on a plate next to the ice bucket, and Ernest cut off hunks with his pocketknife and we shared them with the wine. I could tell from the way he moved his arms to cut the cheese and pour the wine that he was hurting.

Ernest nibbled the Parmesan and sipped his wine for a while, finally said, "When I went back to Paris with my book contract in my pocket I should have gone directly to Schruns, where Hadley and Bumby had been waiting the nineteen days I had been gone. Should have taken the first train from the Gare de l'Est, but Pauline met my boat train when I arrived in Paris. I passed up three trains to stay with her at her place."

He closed his eyes, perhaps seeing himself back then. Time passed. His breathing became deeper. I realized he had fallen asleep.

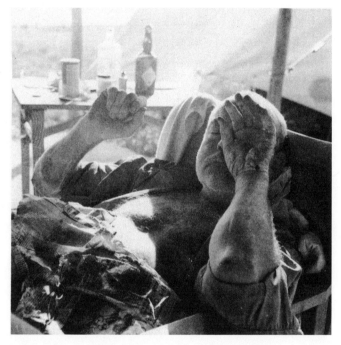

*Ernest suffered multiple injuries after the second consecutive rescue plane crashed in Africa in 1954.*

*Pamplona, Spain, 1926: Sharing a table at the feria are (from left) Gerald Murphy, Sara Murphy, Pauline Pfeiffer, Ernest, and Hadley Hemingway.*

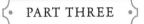

# PART THREE

# Parting of the Ways
# at Harry's Bar

Ernest came to my room late the following morning, bearing the *International Herald Tribune* and several English papers. He said that he had an appointment with a big-shot *dottore* to give him a thorough going-over, roasted scalp to busted sphincter; however, if he was still on his feet maybe we could go to one of his favorite haunts, Harry's Bar, for dinner. In reality it was Cipriani's bar, Harry was simply the Englishman who had backed Cipriani when he opened the bar years back. It was now famous for its Italian specialties as well as its Bellinis. Ernest had known Cipriani since World War I.

They embraced happily and Cipriani escorted us to Ernest's favorite corner table where, as Ernest pointed out, his flanks were well covered. Cipriani, a compact, handsome man with a contagious smile, poured glasses of a shimmering red that came from his own estate.

After he left to attend to his *proprio* duties, a captain appeared to take our orders. Ernest again ordered *fegato alla Veneziana* (as he would at every dinner on our trip), and I opted for linguine *alle vongole*, the minuscule Adriatic clams unknown elsewhere.

"Sorry I nodded off last night," Ernest said. "Where were we?"

"You had passed up three trains for Schruns to stay with Pauline in Paris."

"So I did." He topped off his glass from Cipriani's bottle.

"When I did arrive at the Schruns station, Hadley was standing there, lovely Hadley, and little Bumby, husky and snow-tanned. At that moment I wished I had died before loving anyone else.

"Hadley and I had a happy time that winter in Schruns, skiing and poker games, singing and drinking with the locals at the bar. The Murphys came to visit us, so did Dos Passos, and I thought it had worked itself out and that I was back in safe harbor. I didn't respond to any of her letters.

"But, Christ, soon as we returned to Paris in the spring, I fell back with Pauline who made sure once again I landed in her bed. It went like that all that spring.

When Pauline thought Hadley was getting a little suspicious—she was cagey as hell—she and her sister Ginny invited Hadley to go on a motor trip with them to Châteaux Valley. Hadley was pleased to go since the only places I ever took her were to fish or ski or hunt. I sure as hell didn't take trips just to ride around and gawk at old châteaux.

"While they were away I worked hard and finished revising the book, working on the galleys. It was now ready for publication. I felt free and happy. I expected Hadley to come back from her trip refreshed and friendly toward Pauline, but I was in for something else. When I asked about the trip she said the first few days were fine but then Pauline became testy, rather hostile, cutting off Hadley's attempts at conversation. Hadley said it gave her an uneasy feeling about Pauline and me. So Hadley confronted Ginny, asked her if I was involved with Pauline. Asked her, 'Has Pauline fallen in love with Ernest?' Hadley said that Ginny got nervous, said that Pauline and Ernest were very good friends, and she quoted Ginny's words: 'I think they are very fond of each other.' Hadley said she should have known. That she began to think about those fashion shows for her and those toys for Bumby and 'what an acrobat Pauline is the way she hangs on your every word. When you laugh, she laughs. When you take umbrage, she's your umbragette, the perfect little friend of the family, who as a supreme to-ken of her friendship with the husband . . . I'm so naïve not to have known.'

"Hadley started to cry, said she wanted to save us. Asked if I might get over it if she gave me some time, said there was our son to consider. All of that. Made me angry. Said we were happy just as we were. Said I love you and this shouldn't matter. I wanted to have both of them just as they were, both of them—I didn't know much about women, did I?

"Hadley did hold on for a while, but after some months it wasn't the same with us. We had withdrawn from each other. I was asking too much of her. It was while we were in Pamplona with the Murphys that we decided to split up when we got back to Paris.

"We shared a *lit salon* on the train going back to Paris, knowing that when we arrived at the Gare de Lyon we would go our separate ways. That was a very painful ride. We barely spoke. There was a middle-aged American lady in the compartment traveling with a canary in a cage and she did most of the talking. I was in a kind of daze, as if I'd been floored by a wicked left hook and was trying to clear the cobwebs. Couldn't get my mind to accept the fact that we two who'd lived so close for so long were about to go our separate ways. It was very hot in that compartment. Looked out the window and the passing scene stuck in my eyes, memorizing everything. It was like traveling to an important funeral. It haunted me and eventually I was compelled to write about it in 'A Canary for One.' In my grotesque memory, I saw a farmhouse burning in the field with bedding and things from inside the farmhouse spread out on the field. There were many big advertisements for Belle Jardinière, Dubonnet, and Pernod on walls that went by. We passed tracks with standing cars, restaurant cars and sleeping cars, cars marked Paris-Rome and cars with seats on the roof; I saw cars that had been in a wreck, splintered open, the roofs sagged in. That's how I felt, splintered and sagged, sitting there besides my wife, perhaps for the last time.

"Hadley didn't want to go back to our apartment with all its intimate memories; instead I booked a room for her and Bumby in the Hôtel Beauvoir, across from the Closerie des Lilas. I went to Gerald Murphy's sixth-floor studio at 69 Rue Froidevaux, which he had offered to me. Also, knowing I was broke, he slipped four hundred bucks into my checking account at the Morgan Guaranty, which I used to repay some debts.

"The studio was unheated and I was too strapped to buy *boulets* for the fireplace. The room had an imposing thirty-foot ceiling and walls covered with large oil paintings ranging from six feet to one measuring eighteen by twelve feet—a blend of modernist and Cubist, that were impressive. I could hardly believe the signature of the artist: Gerald Murphy. When I was at his villa in Antibes, the one he later bought and renamed Villa America, I knew he had turned the garage into a studio, but I thought it was just Gerald being a dilettante painter. These paintings, however, were quite wonderful, and they created a fine atmosphere for the room. There was a huge depiction of a watch, its movements overlaying its exterior, and, my favorite, a mélange of a razor, a fountain pen, and a matchbox. There were five paintings in all. Gerald painted for only those seven years of the twenties, fourteen paintings altogether, but afterward those paintings on the wall and the others achieved growing acclaim. They have remained in the museum of my mind.

"I think things started to fall apart with the Murphys when they flattered me into reading aloud from *The Sun Also Rises* to a group of their friends. I thoroughly disliked blowing my own horn, and what's more, I came to realize they were showing me off like a prize horse."

*Schruns, Austria, 1925: Ernest with little Bumby and Hadley during a happy respite from Paris's brutal winter.*

*Pamplona, Spain, 1959: We were picnicking at the Irati River when a gentle hound mysteriously appeared out of the adjoining forest.*

PART FOUR

# La Feria de San Fermín
# in Pamplona

We left Venice for Pamplona the following day and, as arranged, met up with Mary and several of their friends in Pamplona, which is just over the French border in northern Spain. La Feria de San Fermín was seven days and seven nights melted into one, just as Ernest had described it, a raucous drinking, dancing, feasting celebration of the bulls, which ran through the streets every morning and died in the ring every afternoon.

Participating in a complete run of the *feria* certainly heightened my admiration for the way it is depicted in *The Sun Also Rises*, including the afternoon picnics we enjoyed on the banks of the Irati River, so prominent in the book. Ernest captured not only the events but, more important, the emotional nuances that gave the book its thrust.

On one picnic afternoon, high up in the moss-carpeted, beech-wooded forest above the Irati, Ernest was enjoying a brief reprieve from the Pamplona tumult, when a gentle hound dog mysteriously came out of the forest and went over to where Ernest was sitting with his back against a birch tree. I had my camera suspended around my neck and I snapped their picture. Of all the many pictures I took of Ernest over the years, that one was my favorite. The dog settled down next to Ernest and they both closed their eyes and took a little nap together.

One afternoon, while Ernest and I were sitting in choice *barrera* seats in the bullring, waiting for the afternoon's corrida to start, Ernest said that he used to sit in these seats with Lady Duff the first time they came to the *feria*.

"She was a rare one, the Duff was. Specially liked the part where the bull tore up the underbelly of the horse and its guts trailed around under it as the picador went about his business. Of course, horses have protective mattresses now, but not the banderilleros, who, after they stick the barbs, try to vault over the *barrera* before the bull can nail 'em. She loved that chase, always rooting for the bull, and loved it when the bull occasionally hooked the matador in the ass on his way over the fence.

"There was a night here when Duff and I might have gotten it on. There was something about the way she dressed and talked and her utter disregard for convention that was exciting. And yet, that was why it didn't work. At the last moment, she begged off. 'I don't have much in the way of scruples or beliefs or religion,' she said, 'but what I have in place of God is my rock-solid resolution not to fuck married men.'"

Ernest was correct about sleep and the lack of it. Sometimes when it got very late and I was in dire need of closing my eyes, I curled up in the back of the Lancia, which was parked near the central town square. Occasionally Ernest would join me in the front seat.

One night we were invited to a private club where there was a lively band, with everybody singing and drinking the good local wine as they danced. In the small hours of the morning we managed to make our unsteady way to the Lancia. Ensconced in the front seat, Ernest sipped from an uncorked bottle of Navarre red he had carried from the club.

"Damn sight better'n the last one," he said.

"Last one?" I said from the backseat, not reading him.

"Yep. Back in '26 it was a glum *feria* with the Murphys and Hadley. We didn't dance in the street."

"Why glum?"

"I thought Hadley and I had been getting along all right, she putting up with my seeing Pauline, but I found out I was deluding myself. I guess it was the frivolity of Pamplona where everyone was having a good time, that got to her. It was during the next to last bullfight of the *feria* that Hadley said, 'You know something, Ernest, your veronicas have been wearing me down and I want to get out of the ring before it's too late.'

"I pretended not to know what she was talking about, but I knew.

" 'I really can't be someone I'm not.'

"Meaning?

" 'When we get back I'm going to find a separate place for Bumby and me.'

"I wasn't prepared for this. I loved her, and now she was defending her dignity and I couldn't be the one taking it away from her.

" 'You know sometimes the matador gets gored,' I said lamely, 'and if you leave . . .'

" 'I won't go back to the apartment with things as they are. I'm going to leave you at the Gare de Lyon.'

"But we'll be seeing each other. . . .'

" 'No, no good nights after dinner. . . . Once apart . . . well . . . apart.'

"There were tears down her cheeks in the afternoon sunlight. I felt like an intruder had risen up and struck me down."

"Papa, at that moment did it occur to you," I said, "to promise to give up Pauline in order to get Hadley to stay?"

"No, I wasn't ready for this confrontation, and with the commotion of the bullring around me, the olés of the spectators, the blaring music of the band, the performance of the matador on the sand, my head wasn't working. I just accepted what she said as a kind of punishment, especially when she said, 'You well know, Ernest, that when a corrida goes past the time limit, it is called off and the matador and the bull go their separate ways.' "

Ernest drained off the last of his wine. "I told you about going back to Paris in the train compartment the next day, didn't I?"

I said he had.

He put the empty bottle on the floor, and with his head resting against the seat back, he fell asleep.

*In 1932, Ernest went to Havana with his buddy, Joe "Sloppy" Russell, to get away from the Key West house for an extended period and fish for marlin.*

PART FIVE

# Revelations in
# Key West

After Pamplona, Ernest and I stayed in touch with letters and Midgetapes. Ernest's letters were much better than his recordings. The only thing that Ernest feared more than the camera lens was the microphone. Put in front of him, it caused his voice to constrict and his breath to shorten, so he sounded like a long-distance runner halfway through his grind. He was once offered a good deal of money to introduce his stories on television, the network proposing going to Cuba to record him, but after days of suffering over his decision, he announced that his permanent condition of phlegm prohibited his participation.

The next time we actually got together was in the

summer of 1955, to prepare for the first of several televisions plays I was to dramatize from his short stories. I had never written for film or television, but Ernest disliked the "mash-ups" of previous movie and television adaptations. When he asked me to take over all future adaptations, I demurred because I had no experience. He said, "What's that got to do with it? I had no experience writing a novel until I wrote the first one. So, write one script, then you'll have experience."

Ernest suggested that instead of meeting at his Finca Vigía in Cuba, where we had worked on *Across the River*, this time we meet at his house in Key West. Ernest had lived there off and on with Pauline when their sons Patrick and Gregory were growing up, and he taught them fishing and how to shoot and to ride, but he was away on his own adventures, he said, far more than he was in residence.

"I regarded home as a place I left behind in order to come back to it afterward. I fully indulged in trips like the safari to East Africa with three of my friends, accompanied by the celebrated white hunter Philip Percival, who was on all my future safaris. Pauline had gone on my first safari, a deluxe affair paid for by her uncle Gus, and she wanted to join the East Africa group, but I kept the group exclusively male, leaving Pauline to oversee the house and the boys."

On the morning of July 4, 1955, I flew to Miami, caught a small afternoon plane to Key West, and took a taxi to 414 Olivia Street, the address Ernest had given me. It was a street of grimy, run-down houses with ramshackle sidewalk fences and yards with high weeds. When Pauline's uncle Gus had bought this place for Pauline and Ernest in the 1930s, the neighborhood was sparsely settled and the few houses that were there were of a quality that matched Ernest's (actually, he had two houses: a large main house and a small, more modern house beside the pool). The main house was a stone Spanish Colonial with a veranda that featured French windows with green shutters. The lush grounds were covered with sago, palmettos, date palms, and thick banyan trees. The years had not been kind to the neighborhood, and Ernest's house was now an oasis amid squalor. Ernest had not lived there since 1940, when, after a long separation, he was divorced from Pauline; it had become her property as part of the divorce settlement and she had lived there until her recent death, when the property had passed to the children. But the children did not want to live there, nor were they around to look after it. So it fell to Ernest to come over from Cuba, where he lived in the Finca Vigía in San Francisco de Paula to arrange for a broker to rent it or maybe sell it.

Ernest, wearing swim trunks, came from the main house to greet me. He was moving slowly but somewhat better than at the Gritti right after the crash. He settled me into the pool house, and then we both went for a swim in the warm salt water, which had the balming effect of a sulfur bath. Ernest said the pool emptied and filled overnight with semi–salt water. He entered the pool cautiously, stopping several times on the pool steps to splash water across his middle. He swam breaststroke very slowly, with his head out of the water, his frog kick without force, his arms moving through the water listlessly. As he reached each end of the pool, he stopped and rested for several minutes to recharge, no longer the solid swimmer he had been before the plane crash. Mary came down and joined us in the pool.

Mary and Ernest had been invited to an elaborate Fourth of July party, but Ernest had begged off at the last moment and Mary was going alone. Ernest assured her that we could manage in her absence. He consulted his watch. "Past meridian," he said. "We can break out the serious drinks." He took two glasses of scotch and water from the freezer. The water had frozen on top of the scotch, and when you tilted the glass, the scotch cut a rivulet through the ice to reach your mouth, giving the illusion that you were drinking from a mountain stream that had suddenly turned to scotch. I complimented Ernest on his invention.

At dusk, we sat on the terrace as the first pale fireworks invaded the sky. Ernest uncovered slabs of turtle meat that Mary had placed on the table, put them on large slices of pumpernickel bread and slathered them generously with fresh horseradish. It was an absolutely wonderful dinner of mountain-stream scotch and turtle sandwiches.

As dusk fell to night, the fusiliers launched their more spectacular pyrotechnics, the brilliant tracings darting among the low-hanging stars.

"I thought it would be pleasant to get away from the finca," Ernest said, his eyes fixed on the sky, "and to reach into the past for a little peace and solitude. This is where I wrote 'The Snows of Kilimanjaro,' and that's as good as I have any right to be, but now that I'm here, it's not an escape, it just reminds me of a disturbing part of my life. I should have known better than to even hope for redemption."

I sensed this was a good time to ask him what had occurred after he and Hadley went their separate ways. Did he continue seeing Pauline? He said of course, she made sure of that, but he'd kept up his obligation to spend time with Bumby. "On one of those times I came to get him, Hadley intercepted me and said it was time we talked. She asked if I was still fixated with Pauline. Could I give her up? I asked her why she had to stir up all of this. We were happy, weren't we? Why rock the boat? She said if the boat capsized, she was the one who would drown. Only I would have nothing to lose. I said either way, I lose a lot. She picked up a pen and a sheet of paper. 'So there's no misunderstanding,' she said. Then she wrote, 'If Pauline Pfeiffer and Ernest Hemingway do not see each other for one hundred days, and if at the end of that time Ernest Hemingway tells me that he still loves Pauline Pfeiffer, I will, without further complication, divorce Ernest Hemingway.' She signed her name and offered the pen to me. I said it read like a goddamn death warrant. I didn't take the pen. 'It is,' she said. 'Either she dies or I do.' She was right to protect herself with this agreement. Never in my life signed anything with more reluctance. Took the pen and signed.

" 'Then that's it,' she said, taking the paper. 'Bumby and I will go off to live by ourselves until I hear from you. As for not seeing Pauline—you're on your honor.'

" 'Hadley,' I said, 'I love you, I truly do—but this is a peculiar passion I have for her that I can't explain.'

"She said she wasn't asking for an explanation—an explanation really doesn't do much good. She said I was her life, her whole life, and so she was making the sacrifice of her humiliation to try to keep me. 'A hundred days is an eternity, but I will wait it out impatiently, and hope that your peculiar passion will have spent itself.'

"That night I had dinner with Pauline and told her about the hundred days. She smiled and said that was perfectly okay with her, that one hundred days was a short price to pay for getting me. She took a rose from the vase on the table and handed it to me and told me to be sure to press it under our mattress.

"Pauline exiled herself to her hometown of Piggott, Arkansas, population two thousand. Her father and Uncle Gus owned everything there, but their money couldn't alleviate her boredom.

"Before leaving, she left me a message that we were destined to face life together, and that's that. She liked Hadley very much, she wrote, but she was locked out. She said she had the wherewithal for us to live very well, that we could have houses in countries we like all over the world, with servants keeping them open for when we come along with our six or seven sturdy offspring, all of them speaking the language of whatever country we were in. A hundred days is a long time, she wrote, and she didn't relish such a parting, but it will be a parting filled with optimism."

I asked Ernest if Hadley had remained in Paris.

"Yes," he said, "she found an apartment on Rue de

Fleurus, not far from Gertrude Stein's. She gave me a list of the things she wanted from our apartment—furniture, some wedding gifts, heirlooms that had come from her St. Louis family, some clothing, all of Bumby's things, and the painting I had given her for her birthday, an oil by the Spanish artist Miró called *The Farm*.

"I borrowed a handcart from the sawmill people and made several trips to Hadley's place, which was five blocks away from the apartment we were giving up. Putting those intimate things in the cart and pushing them down the street got to me. I started to cry and cried all the way there. Crying is a very rare emotion for me. When I got to her apartment, Hadley wasn't there, Marie Cocotte was minding Bumby, who ran to me happily. When he saw my tears, he asked how I had hurt myself. I showed him a little cut I had on the back of my right hand. He became very concerned and ran to get a bandage that he lovingly placed over the cut, making me cry all the more.

"I put Miró's painting by itself in the last cart. He was a good friend, virtually unknown then. I had to scrimp and borrow to raise its small purchase price. Hadley loved it and hung it on the wall over our bed. Standing on the bed and taking it off the wall and putting it in the cart really punched home what I was doing to myself.

"After I emptied the last cart, I picked up Bumby to

tell him good-bye. He patted my bandage tenderly. 'Je t'aime, Papa,' he said. French was the only language he spoke. 'La vie est beau avec Papa.' "

Ernest got up and took another glass of scotch from the freezer. I still had most of mine. The fireworks kept the sky busy. Ernest tore open a bag of pretzels and dumped them into a bowl.

"I had settled into Murphy's studio," he said, "but I wasn't as keen on the view outside as I was on the paintings inside, since the outside view was of the Cimetière du Montparnasse, which faced the windows. With the cemetery as my vista, and the prospect of one hundred days of misery ahead of me, I was ready for one of the tombstones: Here lies Ernest Hemingway who zigged when he should have zagged."

*Ernest in his saltwater pool in Key West, where I took this picture when I visited him there in 1955.*

PART SIX

# Those to Count On
# and Those to Count Out

On the evening of the third day of my Key West visit, Mary was entertaining members of an elite orchid club who were advising her on how to establish an orchidarium (their word) on the grounds of the finca. That being the case, Ernest decided he and I should get out of the house and get drink and food at his favorite haunt, Sloppy Joe's, Key West's most celebrated saloon.

"I used to be co-owner with Joe Russell of Sloppy Joe's," Ernest said, "'silent partner' they called it. We had gambling in the back and that's where the real money was. But getting good dice changers was difficult because if he was so good you couldn't detect it yourself you knew he would steal from you. The big expense in a gambling operation, ours included, was police protection.

We paid seventy-five hundred dollars to elect a sheriff who in his second year in office went God-happy on us and closed us down, so we closed him down."

The place, with its mementos and rough furnishing, was crowded with tourists, but a protected table in an alcove had been reserved for Ernest. We ordered Papa Doblas, which were copies of the Papa Doblas that had been created for him by the Floridita in Havana. We were also served a heaping plate of unshelled shrimp and a bowl of spicy guacamole.

"Hotch," Ernest said, "I have to ask a favor of you. Miss Mary's been giving me a hard time. Says I'm not the only writer in the family but I'm so damn egoed up I don't pay any attention to her."

"About what?"

"Helping her get assignments. Did you know she was a stringer for *Time* magazine when we first met in London? She wants to write articles. But I don't know how to go about getting her some kind of assignment. I just thought since you're up there in New York where all the magazines are, maybe you could look into it."

I hadn't written for magazines for quite some time and I had lost contact with editors, but I said I would certainly make an attempt. (I did eventually get her an assignment with one of the ladies' magazines, "My Husband, Ernest Hemingway.")

Ernest said he was sorry to ask this of me, "But it is Mary's insistent and without let-up gripe that I have neglected the writer in her, that I don't want her to be competition, on and on, driving me bughouse, on the brink of pitching her typewriter into the drink.

"Martha [his third wife] was just as bad, constantly drumming me about her writing, how we had to make time to fit her schedule, where and when we had to go here and there for her assignments. She was a pretty good writer, I'll give her that, but also as a writer, I wasn't about to put her needs before mine. It was a break to break up, since no children, no love, she was making more money than I was, and she let me know she had a much better future without me. And that was probably right, since our interests and tastes were not the same. I liked the solitude of writing and could not match her in ambition. The fling we had in Madrid during the Spanish Civil War, while the city was being bombed, quickly flung itself out once we made the mistake of getting married, but I have no regrets about the fling since it had the positive effect of finally forcing Pauline to file for divorce."

Now that he was talking about Martha and Pauline, I thought this was a good time to get Ernest back to talking about the hundred days.

"Was *The Sun Also Rises* published by then?"

"Just elbowing its way into the bookstores. Those first

days of my hundred-day sentence, I tried to get my footing by contacting the people I thought I could count on to stand by me, like Lady Duff and her band of fellow tipplers. But when I approached them at the Dôme with inscribed copies of the newly minted *The Sun Also Rises* they turned on me. Pat called me Judas and said they didn't want my stinking book. I said, 'What's eating you? It's only about our Pamplona trip. What's wrong with that?' 'What's wrong,' he said, 'is the whole world now sees me as a pathetic drunk who fucks his promiscuous cousin.' I pointed out that I didn't give the people in the book their names. He said, 'Oh sure, nobody suspects that Lady Duff Twysden is Lady Brett Ashley in the novel? Don't make us laugh.'

" 'Turning me into a vulgar Jew,' Harold said, 'what have I done to make me so malicious? I've boxed with you, played tennis with you, brought you oysters from Prunier, bottles of Pouilly-Fuissé, introduced you to influential people, helped you meet Paris publishers, only to have people everywhere pointing—There goes Harold Loeb, the repulsive Jew in Hemingway's book.'

"I said, 'Listen up, all of you. It's how we were—what we did. I didn't use your real names.' Duff said I got it wrong about her. That she didn't fuck that bloody bullfighter, and then Pat asked if my pecker had been shot off in the war, was I the dickless Jake Barnes?

"I lit into them. 'You goddamn cowards, afraid to face who you are. Pat, you're a mooching drunk who screws his own cousin and sponges off everyone. You, Duff, you're great company, I love you, but let's face it, you hop beds hoping to find some unidentified something you lost. And you, Harold, you know your trouble? You're a Guggenheim with no privileges, frustrated that the other Guggenheims toss you some bones but keep you out of the inner circle, not listening to any of your recommendations.'

"Harold jumped up, overturning his chair, threatening to knock my block off. Duff took over. She told us not to get feisty. Told me I should go and take my books with me. 'We are who we are,' she said. 'We used to be your friends.'

"So that was the sad end of that rooting section. That night I had a liquid dinner of scotch and more scotch at Les Deux Magots."

Ernest signaled the waiter to replenish the daiquiris. Looking at my littered plate, he gave me a puzzled look. "Why'd you leave the shrimp heads? That's the best part." He picked one up and crunched it happily. I crunched one but not happily.

"Word got to me that Harold Loeb had announced that he was going to shoot me on sight for how I wrote about him—that I named him Robert Cohen in the book didn't help. So he would have no trouble finding me, I sent him a telegram, that I'd be in Le Trou dans le Mur at such and such a time on the Boulevard des Capucines, across from the Café de la Paix, but Harold the executioner never showed. However, a week or so later I was having dinner at Lipp's in Saint-Germaine-des-Prés when I spotted Harold entering the restaurant. I went over and extended my hand to him. He smiled and started to shake before he realized that *The Sun Also Rises* had made us mortal enemies. He yanked his hand away and swung it behind his back. I invited him for a drink, but he refused. Actually, 'Never' is what he said. 'Okay,' I said, returning to my table, 'then drink alone.' He left the restaurant, and that was the end of that vendetta.

"The others in that group drifted apart. Perhaps the book had something to do with it. It was very sad about Duff. She got wiped out by a vicious strain of tuberculosis. Her pallbearers had all been her lovers. Leaving the church, one of the grieving pallbearers slipped on the church's old steps and the casket fell and rolled down the steep steps landing on the sidewalk where it split open."

The waiter came to our table and served us what he called a tuna-avocado-crab stack, a little tower of alternating layers, one of Ernest's favorites.

"They watch out for me here," Ernest said. "Did you ever see anything prettier on a plate than this? The cook who invented it committed suicide."

I said it was like no other dish I had ever eaten. We consumed it in silence, giving it our full attention.

"Not bad eating for a saloon," Ernest said when he finished and signaled for a daiquiri replenishment.

I asked him whether his Paris friends took sides over his separation.

"Not so much taking sides as the fact that events took turns kicking me in the ass. Like Gertrude Stein's soirees. I counted on them and on her as a friend. I'd see the artists and writers I knew at those soirees. But there was the evening I'd been having drinks with Picasso at the Dingo. We were discussing the possibilities of his doing illustrations for a book I planned to write on bullfighting. Afterward we went to Gertrude's for one of her weekly gatherings. Jim Joyce, Dos Passos, Janet Flanner of *The New Yorker*, the artist Juan Gris were there when we arrived. While pouring Pablo and me some wine, Gertrude said, 'I hear you two don't like my *Autobiography of Alice Toklas*. My spies told me that you and this other self-appointed critic, Señor Picasso, were at Sylvia's bookstore bad-mouthing it.'

"I said, 'True, we don't like it because it's so full of spiteful lies and malicious character assassination.'

"Gertrude said, 'No, what I wrote was honest criticism of you and everyone else.'

" 'No, lies,' Picasso said.

" 'Those who don't want to swallow bitter truth often reject it as a lie,' Gertrude said.

" 'Lies, Gertrude, lies, full of lies,' I said.

"Gertrude moved her large face close to mine. 'You know, Hemingway, you're someone I created, a macho character who roams the earth looking for adventure. The truth is, under pressure you have proved to be quite yellow, which is really an embarrassment to me.'

" 'Well, gentlemen,' I said, 'what we have here is a mind gone to fat. A woman once in control of whatever faculties she had has now degenerated to nonsensical malaise and self-adulation.'

" 'You're having a little hiccup of success—one book—one drop of water in life's ocean, and that's supposed to qualify you to sit in judgment on one of your betters—don't make me laugh.'

"Joyce now joined the colloquy, saying, 'That's the way to deal with her, Hem. Lies are her staff of life, sitting fatly in her salon, trading her marmalade gossip for crusts of other people's talents. I suggest we leave Gertrude and her lackadaisical libations and adjourn to McGraw's for an honest Irish whiskey.'

"So that was how it ended with Gertrude.

"And then there was the loving letter from my loving mother that I carry next to my heart." Ernest took his billfold from his hip pocket and extracted a tattered slip of paper that he read from: " 'Ernest, I have received the inscribed copy of *The Sun Also Rises,* which you sent to me. Although as your Mother, I am pleased to hear that it is selling well, you have the doubtful honor of having produced one of the filthiest books of the year. Surely you must know some other words besides *damn* and *bitch.* I love you dear and still believe you will do something worthwhile to live after you.' "

Ernest said he had counted on Sylvia Beach and her bookstore as a positive place for him. She was like a sister—in fact, more sisterly than his own sisters—but she was so sympathetic to his predicament, so anxious to comfort him, it made him feel kind of pathetic, and pathetic was what he wanted to avoid. Making it out of this one-hundred-day grinder in one unground piece was what he wanted. So he scratched Sylvia.

"Another thing I counted on was continuing my Thursday nights with Joyce, but when I showed up at our usual watering hole, he let me know that my present predicament put me off-limits for the time being because I was so inundated by my dilemma that my lachrymose disposition watered down his Bushmills.

"It's true that drinking ratcheted up my anguish.

That and the daily letters from Pauline, lamenting the pain and pitfalls of boring Piggott, plus her wild yearning for me, like she wished she could be posted to me in a two-cent plain wrapper. Those letters were fuses that set off lousy, terribly cheap, self-pitying replies from me, wallowing in bathos, blaming myself for her misery, a kind of unsponsored craziness."

I said, "Papa, I thought Joyce was a good friend. I'm sorry to hear he deserted you. What about Fitzgerald?"

"Yes, Scott was really concerned about me. As I was about him. Affectionately criticizing each other was the bond of our friendship. When I described my hundred-day predicament, he was very much on Hadley's side. He said, 'Remember, I tried to keep this from happening. I warned you that Pauline was not content to be your mistress, that she wanted to marry you. Well, last winter she began to move steadily toward nabbing you, but at the same time keeping her contacts with your wife, always presenting herself as an innocent, leaving for a while, but only long enough so that you would miss her. She would probably bring you some positive things, but she would also bring you remorse. Don't try living with remorse—remorse will break your goddamn heart.'

"I told Scott he just didn't understand that loving two women at the same time, honestly loving them, is the worst affliction a man can have. 'Inside me are two men, both happily in love, but twins who cannot live apart—so now one must die—the twins in me share their emotions but have to invent and pretend and evade. You hate yourself for keeping them both alive but you know that one has to die, and yet you have an irrational contentment because two women love you and in a make-believe, irrational fictional world not unlike the ones we create in our novels and stories, an isolated Eden.'

"Scott asked me if they were really different, distinct from each other. I said yes, they were, that Hadley was simple, old-fashioned, receptive, plain, virtuous; Pauline up-to-the second chic, stylish, aggressive, cunning, nontraditional.

"Scott asked if they differed as sex partners.

" 'Night and day,' I told him. 'Hadley submissive, willing, a follower, sweet climax. Pauline explosive, wildly demonstrative, in charge, mounts me, climaxes like a thunderstorm. They're opposites. Me in charge of Hadley and Pauline in charge of me.'

" 'Ernest, listen,' he said, 'the important thing is that *you* should be in charge of *you*. Besides the sex, Pauline is tons of money, servants, fancy apartments, restaurants, first-class safaris, your own boat . . .'

"I said I didn't give a damn for all that.

" 'But you do, Hem,' he said, 'you'll live like I live, something you covet. You'd like to have a regular table at the Ritz, a villa on Cap d'Antibes, top-level safaris. You're tired of poverty. Poverty is grinding and it's worn you down.'

" 'But I'll be making money from my books,' I said.

" 'Not that kind of money,' Scott said. 'You don't have an uncle Gus as your personal banker. You're a piece worker, years between paydays. No money to tide those gaps. You need the shining qualities of Hadley. Her buoyancy. Neither Pauline nor her money can provide that.' "

A couple of decked-out Cuban guys singing to their guitars had been circulating around the saloon. They now arrived at our table and serenaded us with a Cuban song that Ernest knew, and he seemed relieved to toss off his annoying reminiscence and sing along with them. After they moved on, he said he had stored some things in a room in the back of Sloppy Joe's in the thirties, when he left Key West, and he wanted to see if they were still there and in better in shape than the stuff we had seen at the house.

That morning, I had been with Ernest when he opened a door off the living room that led into a room where he had long ago stored first editions, original manuscripts, letters, and unpublished materials. He picked up a first edition of *The Torrents of Spring,* his first published novel, a rare item, and the mildewed cover dropped off in his hand. Inside a small cardboard box was a working manuscript of *To Have and Have Not.* The pages were so stiff and deteriorated, they splintered at his touch. Mildew and jungle rot and evil-chewing beetles had done their dirty work. Ernest said that after he left the scene, Pauline had tidied up. Periodicals that got in the way of housekeeping were pitched. All manuscripts were removed from rotproof file cabinets and packed into cardboard boxes, where they furnished ideal nesting materials for mice and rats and were munched on by the king-size Key West cockroach.

Now in Sloppy Joe's storeroom, Ernest located the rotproof cabinet where he had left his possessions, opened a drawer, and picked up a manuscript of *The Sun Also Rises;* it was in good shape, and so were all the other manuscripts and papers in the drawer. He announced, "How do you like it now, gentlemen? All you beetles and cockroaches go fuck yourselves. No free lunch here." He had a good laugh as he gently shut the drawer. "Sloppy Joe's isn't so sloppy after all," he said.

The following day was very hot, the air static, buzzing squadrons of insects hovering over the garden. Ernest had ordered large blocks of ice, which were floated into the tepid swimming pool, but the effect was more psychological than cooling. We sat on the edge of the shady side of the pool, our legs in the water near the floating ice blocks. Mary was in the living room under the ceiling fan writing letters.

"So you were pretty much alone once the hundred days started?"

"Pretty much. Like being in solitary confinement in a giant jail with no peephole and no key and the jailor being myself. I'd visit Bumby, take him out for a while, usually to the Luxembourg Gardens. Hadley stayed out of the apartment when I came for Bumby, who was adorable, and that made my separation even worse. Bumby invented a name for me—'Madame Papa.' He would tell me about a cruel wolf who lived in the apartment: *'Il n'est pas gentil, le monsieur Loop-Loop.'* Sometimes, when we were not on a Luxembourg bench feeding the pigeons or having ice cream at the pavilion, he'd mention Hadley. *'Mama est triste,'* he'd say. *'Elle pleure.'*

"That really got to me."

A small lizard scudded along the pool's edge, paused on Ernest's kneecap, gave him a quick look and skedaddled on as Ernest continued.

"Trapped in Murphy's unheated studio, broke, down to one scrabbly meal a day, to get my mind away from my misery I goaded myself into writing short stories about painful events in my life. 'A Canary for One' re-created that train ride with Hadley, our last time together, on our way to Paris to set up separate quarters. 'In Another Country' took me back to the Ospedale Maggiore in Italy, where I took therapy for my busted knee alongside an Italian major whose right hand had been mutilated. Writing about them helped to purge those painful memories.

"Some nights, instead of trying to sleep but flunking, I wandered around Paris. I'd hang around the Place Concorde, with its swirling traffic, or sit at a café near the Arc de Triomphe drinking scotch and watching the panorama of the Champs-Elysées.

"Sometimes I hallucinated, reliving fragments, like the day Hadley told me she was pregnant and I held her and said I could determine if it was a boy or girl. I lowered her to the floor and got my old lucky rabbit's foot out of my pocket, the fur pretty far gone from years of good-luck rubbing. I told her to lie very still as I suspended the rabbit's foot over her face. If it moved left, it's a girl; right, it's a boy. We held our breath as the foot moved gently to the right. Hadley giggled and jumped up and said, 'Let's celebrate—buy a paper cone of fries and sausages from the vendor on the corner and go picnic in the Tuileries.'

" 'It's snowing.'

" 'All the better—we can throw snowballs at the statues.'

" 'I love you, kitten.'

" 'Will you love me forever?'

" 'Through infinity.'

" 'I don't know much about infinity.'

" 'Infinity begins where forever leaves off.'

" 'Oh, yes, please—infinity.'

"There were severe nights, doomed and bottomed out, I dumped myself into the lower dregs, like the rancid Café des Amateurs, a cesspool on the Rue Mouffetard, packed with hopeless drunks, reject whores, petty thieves, and failed pimps; perhaps lowering myself to their depth was a way of chastising myself for blackening my soul."

Ernest stopped, a pained look from the remembrance on his face. He reached down and scooped up water beside an ice block and doused his chest and the back of his neck. He sat like that for a while, the thrumming insects the only sound. I thought that was the end of his recollection. But he lowered himself into the shallow water and continued. "Those were the times I seriously considered suicide. Not the obvious slitting wrists or gas jets from which you could be rescued. Maybe checking out while I slept, but how? Or some way while skiing, like having my heart stop while running straight down in fresh powder, or an avalanche, but suffocation would be a nasty way to go. I went skiing for a few lonely days and discussed suicide by avalanche with Fräulein Glaser at the Hotel Taube. She told me stories about the deaths of people killed in avalanches, which convinced me it was not a good way to go.

"I decided the best way would be to jump off an ocean liner at night. All you need is the courage to jump. That would be easy for me, since I like to dive. There would be no postmortem. Just a disappearance. It would absolve Pauline of sin, Hadley would avoid having to divorce me, and Bumby would be told angels came to get his papa.

"Those suicidal spasms didn't last for long, but the hundred days continued to hang over my head like an andiron. One of the places I found some solace was the church of Saint-Sulpice. Twin towers, three tiers of elegant columns, massively delicate. Almost as big as Notre Dame, but more comforting. Located just beyond the Jardin Luxembourg. Passed it many times with Hadley and Bumby in his stroller, but its being Catholic, we never went for services. But now I went quite often. Not to pray, although Pauline, who was devotedly Catholic, tried to indoctrinate me, but what induced me now was the old, faded inscription over the main entrance, eulogizing the Superbeing, plus the immortality of the soul. Since I devoutly believed in the immortality of my soul, I felt at home there. I had written a story, 'Now I Lay Me,' that reflected on how, after I was blown up at night in the war, I felt my soul go out of me and then come back.

Now having offended my soul, I was loath to sleep because I feared if I shut my eyes in the dark, my soul would again slip out of my body and go off but, with good luck, come back. So my soul and I would visit one of the small, beautiful chapels inside Saint-Sulpice, especially when the giant organ was playing. Probably the largest, most elegant in the world. It towered against one wall and produced wonderful, overwhelming music that fed my soul and sustained me for days after hearing it."

Mary called us for lunch, served on the veranda. Ernest said it was too hot to eat, but he got out of the pool, dried off, went up to the veranda, and sat down at the table.

After lunch, which featured Mary's recipe for cold fruit soup, we went for siestas, Ernest and Mary going to the main house, with its outside metal staircase that led to their bedroom on the second floor, and I to the guest house which mercifully had a ceiling fan (Ernest was adamantly opposed to air conditioning). I tried to siesta but I'm not good at it. I spent some time watching a sizable scorpion explore the area around the bed.

I went back to the veranda, where a corps of dragonflies was dancing over the pool. Ernest eventually joined me, bearing two wine spritzers. I reminded him that before lunch he had been telling me about the hundred days.

"Those black days," he said, shaking his head. "I marked them off my calendar the way a convict marks his. The nights were particularly bad, but some places helped take my mind off them. One of them was Le Jockey, a classy nightclub in Montparnasse—wonderful jazz, great black musicians who were shut out in the States but welcomed in Paris. I'd sit at the bar. Beautiful women on the dance floor. Wonderful New Orleans jazz. Saxophones, horns, drums like I'd never heard. One of those nights, I couldn't take my eyes off a beautiful woman on the dance floor—tall, coffee skin, ebony eyes, long, seductive legs: Very hot night, but she was wearing a black fur coat. She was dancing with a big British army sergeant, but her eyes were on me as much as my eyes were on her. I got off my bar stool and cut in on the Brit who tried to shoulder me away but the woman left the Brit and slid over to me. The sergeant looked bullets at me. The woman and I introduced ourselves. Her name was Josephine Baker, an American, to my surprise. Said she was about to open at the Folies Bergère, that she'd just come from rehearsal.

"I asked why the fur on a warm night in June. She slid open her coat for a moment to show she was naked. 'I just threw something on,' she said; 'we don't wear much at the Folies. Why don't you come? I'm headlining as the ebony goddess.' She asked if I was married. I said

I was suspended, that there were two women, one my wife, and neither wanted to compromise.

" 'We should talk,' she said. She'd once had a situation like that.

"I proposed that we go have a drink where the saxophone wasn't curdling our ears. She agreed but thought the Limey sergeant might cause a bit of a ruckus. She was right. The Brit did try to stop us from leaving. 'She came with me,' he said, 'and she leaves with me.' I said, 'That's for the lady to decide.' The Brit said he'd be waiting for me outside.

"As we left the Jockey, the sergeant grabbed my arm, tearing off my sleeve, spun me, and knocked me against the wall. I came back at him; we had a tough exchange, police whistles on the way. I was getting the better of him and dropped him as the police whistles closed in. Josephine grabbed my sleeve from the ground and pulled me away.

"I spent that night with Josephine, sitting at her kitchen table, drinking champagne sent by an admirer. I carried on nonstop about my trouble, analyzing, explaining, condemning, justifying, mostly bullshit. Josephine listened, intense, sympathetic; she was a hell of a listener. She said she, too, had suffered from double love.

" 'I fear for my soul,' I told her. 'Either way I go, I hurt one of my ladies, and that's bad for my soul. It nearly left me once and now I was afraid that what I was doing would offend my soul and drive it from me, never to return. I asked her how she thought I might dissuade my soul from condemning me.

"Josephine took her time answering. She said she felt about her soul the way I felt about mine. That the only praying that she did was for her soul, that her soul was her religion. 'It's true,' she said, 'cruel vibes can offend the soul and send it on to a better place. You need some good stuff to happen in your life, Ernie, to rescue you with your soul.'

"The rest of that night, into dawn, we talked about our souls, how I could convince my soul that despite my rejection of one of these women and inflicting hurt on her, it shouldn't reject me."

I said I remembered him writing about Le Jockey and the fight with the British sergeant in one of his stories, but the girl wasn't Josephine Baker.

"No," he said, "I thought her feeling about the soul was her private business, so I invented a woman to take her place in the story and I left out everything about the soul. I never use actual names in what I write. I wrote about Scott, for example, but I gave him a cover name: Julian [in "The Snows of Kilimanjaro"].

"One of my favorite haunts on my sleepless nights was the familiar confines of the Jardin Luxembourg. I'd go there to hear concerts in the open-air bandstand, an elevated century-old enclosure of metal filigree and weaves. I'd hang on after the concert ended, when a few musicians would stay and improvise, and the *locateur* of the pavilion would provide sparkling white wine in defiance of closing hours. It helped that the gendarme on duty was his brother-in-law. On one occasion, though, there was a substitute gendarme for the brother-in-law, and when I refused to leave the Jardin, I was given a summons for loitering.

"Some nights I went to the Jardin very late and slept on a garden bench under my favorite stand of chestnut trees in the lee of my favorite fountain.

"On one night that was particularly bad, I went to the far end of the Luxembourg where it gives onto Rue de Tournon. There's the original small bronze working model of the Statue of Liberty there, her torch a few feet higher than my head, the bronze plaque attached to the base identifying it."

"On this night, as on other nights when I was beginning to feel an urge to bail out and go back to the States, it helped spending some time with this familiar lady. When I got like that I sometimes visited her for her blessing, just as churchgoers visit their favorite saint.

"This particular night, I was feeling a kind of resentment for my predicament, a sort of panic, placing the blame on Paris intrigue, not my own doing.

"I sat there on a bench facing Lady Liberty and took myself back to Oak Park and the day I left our house and the smothering nagging of my mother and lit out on my own with nothing but my own determination to keep me going. I was nineteen, half adventurous, half scared. Getting to Italy and the glory of being an officer in the middle of combat [World War I], but then right off the bat blown up in a trench eating a cheese sandwich, the hospital and rehabilitation in Milan and beyond, limping back to Oak Park, rejected by the nurse I thought I was going to marry, stuck in that house with that righteous Bible-quoting mother of mine.

"So now, I thought, maybe I should once again limp

back to the States and come down off my literary high horse and give up this conceit that I belong here, where I have made such a goulash of my life and the lives of those I really care about. How pathetic that I've been seriously thinking about suicide as the only way out. I said all that to Lady Liberty, and in the saying I realized what a coward I had become.

"The Luxembourg helped me through several nights like that, and the new day would come along and reset my clock.

"One night, after a string of bad nights, I decided to visit my original neighborhood where we lived at 74 Rue du Cardinal-Lemoine in a small two-room flat, a steep four-flight walk-up. I stood across from our scabrous building, which had a water faucet and a pissoir on every landing but not in our flat. Our bathroom was a closet that had only a pitcher, a bowl, and a slop jar that had to be emptied into a big slop jar on the landing below. Garbage was four flights down into a big garbage bin in the courtyard.

"Thinking about that drab place, I was reminded of my constant hunger. We'd been living on less than less— one egg each or a boiled potato for lunch. Sometimes I'd grab a pigeon in the Luxembourg for dinner.

"No nostalgia for that time of my life, I can tell you. On the street level next door was a *bal musette*, which was just as lively as it had been when I lived there, the same sign above its entrance: CAROINEL CLUB DANSE. I crossed the street and went in and ordered a whiskey at the bar. It was the same dim, smoky, crowded place, with couples closely dancing on the narrow floor. Had the same mix of workingmen, sailors, and apaches, who whirled their women around the dance floor in a kind of acrobatic fox-trot, mixed with torrid tango-like sweeps, twirls, twists, and dips. At the end of the bar was an assortment of ladies, *poules* among 'em, who were available to dance for tokens bought from the bartender.

"As before, there was an accordion player on a little platform churning out perky music, hyping the rhythm by stomping his boot, a circle of bells wound around his ankle.

"I had several whiskies and thought about things. After a while, I bought a token and chose a girl who had bad red hair and a good smile. We danced and she held her hand on the back of my neck and her full breasts fastened onto me. Her cheap perfume didn't bother me. I asked her to leave with me and she was willing, but when we got to the door I backed off, gave her a few francs, and left by myself.

"I hailed a taxi and went to a Turkish bathhouse I knew, wrapped myself in towels and slept in the steam room until dawn."

*Horton Bay, Michigan, September 3, 1921: Ernest and Hadley's wedding day, attended by Ernest's sister, Ursula, his mother, and his little brother, Leicester.*

PART SEVEN

# The End of the
# Hundred Days

After dinner that evening in Key West, Mary decided we should go to the movies, but Ernest declined on the grounds that he couldn't sleep after being air-conditioned because of what it did to his circulatory system. Ernest was always protecting himself against a considerable array of potential physical assaults, particularly in the kidney area. His precautions had intensified since the crashes.

After Mary departed, Ernest suggested we walk the beach to a favorite bar that was perched over the ocean. It was a good rustic place, with the moon overhead glinting off the water, and a wizard guitar player entertaining wordlessly. Ernest drank the house wine and I drank beer.

When the guitar player took a break, I picked up where we had left off earlier in the day.

"So, Papa," I said, "what happened when the hundred days ended?"

"It didn't."

"Didn't what?"

"The end started on the seventy-first day that I marked off my calendar. That morning, Hadley asked me to take care of Bumby while she made a trip to Chartres. You know Chartres?"

I said I didn't.

"You need to go, ancient place on the bank of the Eure River, only sixty miles from Paris, thirteenth-century Gothic cathedral, stained-glass windows like no others. Hadley and I had meditated there and walked the cathedral's difficult labyrinth, four quadrants to reach the rose at the center. I guessed she was going to stay where we had stayed, the Hôtel de la Ville. I spent the days with Bumby and delivered him to Marie Cocotte at night. He was a joy. We went to the zoo and the Cirque d'Hiver but mostly to the Jardin Luxembourg, with its playgrounds and merry-go-round.

"A few nights after Hadley had gone to Chartres, I was having a drink at the Dingo Bar, talking prizefighting with the bartender, Jimmy Charters, a Liverpool Limey who had once been a featured lightweight boxer.

I was using the Dingo as my mail drop, and on this night he handed me my accumulated mail. One envelope had Hôtel de la Ville on it; my breath caught in my throat. Why would Hadley write to me? I dreaded opening it. I took my knife from my pocket, unclasped the blade, slid it carefully along the flap of the envelope, and unfolded the single sheet of stationery inside. It began 'Dear Ernest,' Hadley's handwriting, only a few lines. It said although thirty days short of the time she had set, she had decided to grant me the divorce I obviously wanted. Although she had taken me for better, for worse that didn't include marrying someone else. She was now just a friend. She was not going to wait any longer for my decision, which she felt was obvious. She was granting me the freedom I wanted. I reread the letter several times, letting it soak in. All those frantic lovesick letters I wrote to Pauline—why wasn't I feeling some kind of joy now, instead of a kind of numbness? This brief letter, not in actual words, but nevertheless exuding pain, surrender, loss, all my doing. I carefully refolded the letter and put it in the inside pocket of my corduroy jacket and left the Dingo, Jimmy's words following me: 'You didn't finish your drink, Mr. Hemingway.'

"I needed to walk. There was a late-rising moon. I crossed the Boulevard du Montparnasse and took the Rue Guynemer to the narrow Rue Bonaparte, which led me to the Seine. I was not seeing anything or thinking anything. At the balustrade I watched boats and barges navigating the Seine below me; then I went down the stone steps onto the Quai Malaquais where I was level with the river. There was a single fisherman smoking a pipe, trying his midnight luck. I found a stone bench against the wall of the quai and watched the river traffic from there. My numbness slowly gave way to the reality of her letter. I suppose that down deep I had been unrealistically hoping that when the hundred days were up Hadley would decide to go along with my desire to keep both of them in my life. Maybe that illusion is what kept me going, kept me writing those unhinged notes to Piggott. But Hadley's terse, stark letter, giving up on me, made me feel her pain, her exclusion, the loss I had inflicted on her, and my thoughts became very concerned about my soul. This was a cruelty to my soul, the very thing Josephine and I had talked about, how important our souls were, and how somehow I had to redeem my soul or suffer it deserting me.

"As the night wore on, I began to get drowsy, but I forced myself to stay awake, to keep watch that my soul did not leave me. To keep awake I did what I had done years ago in the Italian army when I had faced this predicament. I kept my mind centered on my boyhood: hunting in the woods with my father who gave me only three cartridges for my rifle; listening to a Cubs game with my buddy Bill while filching some of his father's whiskey; fishing for trout when I came back from the war and reliving the best catches; those times in the woods with the Indian girl Prudy Bolton; the painful arguments with my God-fearing Mother; those nights when nurse Agnes von Kurowsky, who I stupidly hoped to marry, came to my bed in the hospital; my sister Geraldine's wedding; the things that happened when I was nineteen and bummed my way to New York, especially that night the brakeman busted me off the freight and at the railroad tracks I met up with a crazy prizefighter and his big black keeper; the five whores at the railroad station, waiting for the train, the really big one, Alice, who must have tipped the scales at three hundred and fifty, as big as three women, had a pretty face and bragged about being laid by the champ prizefighter Steve Kechel.

"I was relieved when the dawn finally broke over the Seine, chasing the enemy night away and bringing more traffic on the river. The midnight fisherman had gone but others began establishing their places on the Seine's abutment. I raised my cramped, tired body from the bench and went back up the old worn stone steps, heading for Murphy's studio. It was imperative that I make a move to pacify my soul. I sat down at the desk under

Murphy's giant watch painting, began to write a letter to Hadley. I complimented her brave and generous reaction and told her I was now informing Scribner that all of my royalties from *The Sun Also Rises* should go to her. I admitted that if I hadn't married her I would never have written this book, helped as I was by her loyal and loving backing and her actual cash support. I told her that Bumby was certainly lucky to have her as his mother. That I had great admiration for her head, her heart and lovely hands, and prayed that God would take care of her to make up for the hurt I had inflicted on her. That she was the best and honest and loveliest person I had ever known. I folded the letter, put it in an envelope that had Murphy's return address, consciously ran the glue of the envelope's flap across my tongue and carefully sealed the flap. I had achieved the moment I had tenaciously sought, but I wasn't elated, nor did I send a cable to Pauline. What I felt was the sorrow of loss. I had contrived this moment, but I felt like the victim.

"I picked up another piece of stationery and I wrote to Pauline, telling her the swell news that Hadley had capitulated and that she could now come back to Paris."

Shortly after his letter to Hadley, Ernest said, he received a return letter from her, thanking him for giving her and Bumby all the royalties from *The Sun Also Rises* but also asking him to remove the suitcases he had been storing in her dining room.

"She ended with a kind and maternal mantra that I be sure to eat well, sleep well, keep well and work well. She signed off with 'Mummie's love.' That really touched me."

*Ernest on the beach with Pauline in 1927.*

# PART EIGHT

# For Whom the
# Wedding Bell Tolls

We left the bar soon after the guitarist returned, and on our way back to Ernest's house I asked him what happened when Pauline returned to Paris.

"It was my expectation," Ernest said, "that I would vacate Murphy's studio and move to Pauline's apartment on Rue Picot when she came back to Paris, which I did, and that we would finally have time to enjoy the freedom of openly living together, but we had never discussed marriage, and certainly I wasn't of a mind to rush into it without a decent transition, if at all. But not Pauline. She immediately booked a church for the wedding, fashionable Saint-Honoré d'Eylau in the Place Victor Hugo. A big wedding with all the pomp of a fancy church certainly wasn't something I wanted. Nor the finest gold-embossed wedding announcements she ordered from Cartier nor the hunt for a 'grand apartment that suits us.'" Ernest said he never liked to be crowded and he felt the need to take a deep breath. So, he said, he got in touch with his good friend Guy Hickok, Paris bureau manager for the *Brooklyn Daily Eagle*, who had suggested they do a tour of Mussolini's fascist Italy.

"I informed Pauline that Guy and I were going on a ten-day bachelor tour of Italy for the Promotion of Masculine Society, but she didn't find it amusing since it forced her to move her church reservation a month later.

"Guy and I set off in his thirdhand two-seater Ford coupe, entering Italy at Ventimiglia and haphazardly stopping in Pisa, Florence, Bologna and other places I decided were bachelor-friendly. I wrote about the trip in a story I called 'Che Ti Dice La Patria?' Those good ten days batted down the wedding pressure.

"But not for long. When I returned to Paris I was confronted with a couple of things that brought me back to reality. To begin with, Pauline informed me that not being a Catholic I couldn't be married in Saint-Honoré d'Eylau Church, meaning that in the two weeks before the wedding I had to prove I was what I wasn't. Not that I had anything against being a Catholic. Pauline was devoutly Catholic—in fact, there was a little chapel in the Piggott house—and I had gone to Catholic churches with her while she prayed, but my only sort of Catholic connection, if you could call it that, was that I loved Mantegna's painting of Jesus on the cross, *Dead Christ*, and other such images of Jesus on the cross. But as for me actually being a Catholic, the best I could do was to try to convince the church elders that when I had been wounded in Italy and transported to a dressing station, where I was lined up with other wounded, a priest from the Abruzzi anointed us while walking along the row of beds.

"On top of the Catholic aggravation, there was a notice waiting for me that my divorce from Hadley was final. I don't know why, but that deeply disturbed me, even though it was to be expected.

"It was during the time I was being interrogated by the church that I ran into a problem that resulted in making my explanation about my Catholicism more convincing. The problem was, I had not been able to have sex with Pauline. A problem I had never had before— trying, but nothing doing. Pauline was all right about it, but I finally had to bring it up. 'I'm as bad as Jake Barnes,' I told her. 'He had a good excuse—his pecker shot off in the war. What's my excuse?'

"She said maybe it was her fault, being so busy with the wedding plans and not doing enough for me when we got in bed. 'No,' I said, 'you've been very good, not being upset or mentioning it, but how do you explain it, since we were so terrific when I was with Hadley?' She asked if I'd seen a doctor. I said I had and I had also tried all kinds of inducements like Spanish Fly, Chinese potions, a variety of pills, electrodes fastened to my testicles. 'Maybe you shouldn't be marrying damaged goods,' I said.

"She hated to see me suffer, she said, so would I do something for her? How about going to church and praying?

"I said praying was okay for her, since she was a good Catholic, but I wasn't a religious anything and I didn't have any standing.

" 'God hears.'

"Also, I'd feel kind of foolish getting down on my knees and asking Jesus to give me an erection.

" 'There's a little Catholic church two blocks from here. Give it a try. What have you got to lose?'

"I was desperate, so I went. The little church had a side altar with a statue of the Virgin Mary, where there were two nuns praying. Feeling foolish, I went to the altar and knelt self-consciously in front of the Virgin, keeping my eye on the nuns who were not paying any attention to me. I spoke to the Virgin in a whisper: 'Holy Mother,' I said, 'I'm not a member in good standing, but my woman is, and on her behalf I have a request. I'm a male, as you can see, and it's my job, I'm the one to plant the seed, but to plant the seed I need a strong hoe. I once had a good hoe, Virgin Mary, but not now, so in the name of your son Jesus and the Holy Ghost, grant me a strong hoe so I can plant my seed. Amen.'

"I went back to the apartment. Pauline was waiting in bed. She rolled on top of me and we had as good a session as we'd ever had.

"From then on I was more enthusiastic promoting my Catholicism with the church elders."

When we reached the house, Ernest made drinks and we continued talking on the terrace.

"I think I told you, Pauline was desperately looking for an apartment much grander than the one I had with Hadley. She urged me to help her look, but I flatly refused. I was not yet ready for any of this hurried bullshit. There was a flood of one-thousand-dollar wedding checks coming in from the extended Piggott clan (many of the presents Hadley and I had received were family heirlooms, but Piggott didn't have heirlooms), plus a smattering of Lalique china and Jensen silver, which, of course, would never be used.

"I made my regular visits to Hadley's apartment to pick up Bumby for our scheduled times together. Hadley usually absented herself when I arrived, but one time she was still there when I arrived. We had a very nice rather affectionate talk and, to my surprise, not having planned it, there suddenly blurted out of me that if she wanted me I would like to go back to her. She smiled and said things were probably better as they were. Afterward, I spent some time at the Dingo Bar berating myself.

"Without any input from me, Pauline did succeed in finding an apartment on Rue Férou that measured up to her requirements. It had a formal living room, spacious master bedroom, dining room, full-size kitchen, two bathrooms, maid's room and a study. Obliging uncle Gus was only too happy to pay for it, as he would be for our automobile, house in Key West, my fishing boat, and our deluxe twenty-five-thousand-dollar African safari.

"For the wedding, Pauline wore a dress designed for her by Lanvin, a strand of Cartier pearls, and a hairdo sculptured close to her head. For my part, I wore a tweed suit with a vest and a new necktie."

I asked Ernest if any of his friends who had deserted him during the one hundred days came to the wedding.

"No," he said, "I didn't invite them."

Mary came on the terrace, returning from the movie.

"So, Kintner," Ernest said, using one of his affectionate names for her, "how was the flick?"

"Gable was too old for the part. He ought to hang it up," she said petulantly, like she'd been defrauded.

"You can't fool the bloody camera," Ernest said sympathetically. "How about a swim, get your mind off it."

"I don't want to take a swim," Mary said emphatically. "I'm going to bed. You and Hotch have a nice evening?"

"We had drinks at Swan's."

"There's fresh pineapple in the fridge. You like pineapple, Hotch?"

I said I did. She uncovered a tin of cookies she said went very well with the pineapple. Then she said "Good night" and went to bed.

"She's very finicky about movies," Ernest said. "Hard to please." He broke a cookie in half and shared it with me. "Let's skip the pineapple." He got up and put a record on the player. It was a chanteuse singing a throaty song in French.

"We were talking about your wedding at the Saint-Honoré d'Eylau Church," I said. "Did you have music?"

"Just huffy stuff from the organ."

"I'll bet you were more than ready for your honeymoon."

I knew that for their honeymoon, Ernest had chosen

the primitive, secluded village of Grau-du-Roi, a place we had visited for lunch when he and I were driving the Grand Corniche on our way to Pamplona. Grau-du-Roi is a few miles below the walled city of Aigues-Mortes, at the bottom of the Rhone estuary. Ernest clearly loved this place and I could see why as we probed the wonderful ramparts that Ernest said were built in the thirteenth century by Simone Bocanegra to protect Aigues-Mortes, also where King Louis IX launched his crusade. Ernest said he chose Grau-du-Roi for the honeymoon to purge the grand pomposity of the Paris church by staying in a modest pension, walking the long white beach, swimming in the unhurried water, and eating the simple food of the village.

Ernest said it was also a grand place to write. He had told Pauline he'd be working in the mornings and that afternoons would be for fishing and swimming and walking the long, picturesque beach. "I felt good about two stories I wrote there," he said, " 'Ten Indians' and 'Hills like White Elephants,' but there was a bad spell I did not feel good about, when I was again upset by being impotent, not exactly what a bride's groom should bring to a honeymoon. But Pauline shrugged it off. Whatever I did or didn't do was all right with her. She had gone through hell to get me and she treated me like a prize from a box of Cracker Jack."

*Kujungu Camp, Tanganyika, Africa, 1934: The all-male safari that deliberately ex-cluded Pauline: Ben Fourie, Charles Thompson, Philip Percival, and Ernest with their kudu and oryx antlers.*

*Pauline sometimes trimmed Ernest's hair during his periodic returns to Key West.*

# PART NINE

# The Short Unhappy Life
# of the Pfeiffer Nuptial

The following day in Key West, Ernest didn't appear until late afternoon, when we finally got around to the purpose of my visit: Ernest's stories that I was scheduled to adapt for television. One of the stories in particular, "The Gambler, the Nun, and the Radio," had very little meat on its bones and I needed more input from him.

Ernest was very helpful, and when we finished I was a bit more confident about tackling the stories. He poured us drinks "to cool out."

Mary came to the terrace accompanied by a short Cuban woman who was carrying a large dish that she put before us. "Carmilito fried you some calamari to have with your drinks," Mary said. "We're going to Teddy's to pick up rock lobsters and pompano for dinner. Anything else, hon?"

"How about shimmy rice with the pompano?"

Mary asked Carmilito if she knew how to make shimmy rice. I, for one, had never heard of shimmy rice, but Carmilito had, and off they went.

Ernest held up his glass. "Here's to shimmy rice," he said. We sipped our scotch and nibbled on the calamari which was tender and crisp. The sun had gone down and it was not so hot.

"You ever read that old bugger Nietzsche?" he asked.

"A little," I said.

"You know what he said about love? Said it's a state where we see things widely different from what they are."

"Pauline?"

"Yup. It didn't take long to unsee those things. I guess it started when we went to live with her folks in Piggott. During our honeymoon in Grau-du-Roi I had been thinking about a new book. A lot of books were being written about the First World War we had fought against the Germans in France and Germany, but I had a monopoly on Italy and the part of the war I was in there. I started the book in Grau-du-Roi and afterward wrote early every morning in Piggott before the suffocating heat took over. The days and nights were as bleak as a stretch of Sahara Desert. Evenings with the Pfeiffers were painfully boring, and Pauline, who seemed to enjoy the after-dinner banality, did nothing to help me escape them. There was nothing in Piggott to relieve the bone-crushing monotony. The only hunting was for quail, and that was out of season, and there was no water for fishing. I wrote on my new book from dawn to noon, when the temperature was less forbidding, but from noon on there was just Piggottry.

"The gloom intensified when I received a letter from Fitzgerald telling me that Hadley had remarried with Paul Mowrer, a journalist I knew. Gentle, thoughtful man, he was Paris correspondent for the *Chicago Daily News.* Letter said they were going to live in a country place near Crécy-en-Brie, outside Paris. What threw me was how quickly Hadley had married. I should have known that her attractiveness and wonderful personality would encourage suitors, but my fantasy was that she would still be single when, as it seemed more and more likely, I would leave Pauline and return to her and Bumby. I had been writing her affectionate letters since the divorce, writing to her close to the line, telling her that the more I saw of members of her sex, the more I admired her. In fact, in all my letters I told her how much I still loved her. I continued to write her after her marriage, as intimate as I dared, but Hadley finally wrote me that my letters were a bit upsetting to Paul, so I stopped writing her from then on.

"As depressing as existence was in Piggott, it got even worse when Pauline announced she was pregnant. Just as marriage had reared up too soon, so was I not ready for the upset of having a baby around. And a helleva upset it turned out to be. We had gone to Kansas City to facilitate the birth, but Pauline had a horrendous battle in the delivery room for eighteen grueling hours that surrendered to a cesarean operation.

"I had previously been through an easy delivery with Hadley, but with Pauline there were serious complications from the very beginning, her labor was brutal, and she screamed with the pain even though the doctor injected her. I was having a different memory pain because of the time with my father when that Indian woman was screaming just like this. My father, who was a doctor, was going up the lake to an Indian camp to attend to a pregnant Indian woman who was in serious trouble. He took me along with him in the boat that was being rowed up the lake. I was a young boy then, maybe seven or eight. My father explained to me that the woman had been trying to have her baby for very many hours but it couldn't make it out of her. He explained that babies should come out of their mother headfirst but if the baby's not in the right position, they have to be cut out of the mother's belly, but he said he didn't have proper instruments so he'd have to use his pocketknife. I tried not to look, but I did see the baby when my father took him out and held him up. And now after eighteen hours of suffering like that Indian woman, they were going to cut Pauline open to cesarean the baby. That poor Indian woman haunted me for a long time. But I thought that long afterward, when I wrote about it in 'Indian Camp,' and about her husband, who killed himself in the bunk above her, I had worked it out of me, but that terrible ordeal with Pauline brought it all back.

"It took us twenty-one hours in a brutally hot and humid train, the baby squalling all the way, to return to Piggott, and I was fit to be shot from a cannon to get away. So to spring myself from the Piggott internment, I got in touch with an old friend, Bill Horne, met up with him in Kansas City, and drove to a dude ranch in Wyoming, where, praise the Lord, I had a really good three weeks away from Pauline, the squalation, and the Piggott clan. I worked mornings on my new book, *A Farewell to Arms,* fished for trout and hunted for grouse in the afternoons, and at night dined on good ranch vittles and good bootleg whiskey.

"After three weeks, Pauline left the baby, named Patrick, with her sister, Ginny, and showed up at the ranch. Leaving Patrick with Ginny for long stretches became so frequent that Ginny was often taken to be his mother. Pauline gamely tried to fish and shoot and ride but she wasn't good at it, not nearly as skilled as Hadley had been on horseback and with rod and gun. I began plans to go on an African safari, but when Pauline heard about it, she took over and got her ever-obliging uncle Gus to sponsor a twenty-five-thousand-dollar deluxe safari. She was not good at tracking and shooting big game, but she gamely tried to keep up for my sake, not because she enjoyed the hunt. I went on several more safaris after that one, but not with Pauline, and not deluxe."

Mary and Carmilito returned and brought some cracklings to occupy us while they prepared dinner.

"You often eat this royally?" I asked Ernest.

"Hell no. Mary's showing off for you."

The cracklings were delicious.

"I'll tell you when I threw in the towel on Pauline," Ernest said, "when she announced she was going to have another baby. The first one had made me bughouse and a second one, howling and spewing, would finish me off. And it nearly did. This time there were twelve hours of battle before the doctor mercifully performed another cesarean. Afterward, the doc took me aside and confided that this had to be her last pregnancy and that from then on I had to do coitus interuptus when we had sex. That's all I needed. The baby was another boy—this one we named Gregory—even more of a howler and squaller than Patrick, so, as before, I got out of Piggott fast. This time I went to Key West to meet up with my old buddy Joe Russell—I told you he and I once were co-owners of Sloppy Joe's—for a two-week spell in Cuba. Joe kept his boat, the *Anita*, docked in Havana. Actually, the two weeks stretched to two months. I rented a corner room at the Ambos Mundos Hotel in Havana. Joe and I spent most mornings going out for marlin.

"Havana was a terrific night town back then with flashy nightclubs, wide-open gambling tables in the hotels, dance *academias* with attractive girls who charged five cents a dance, fluctuating betting at the jai alai *frontón*, amusement halls with dance groups and musicians, plus the Floridita bar and restaurant with its margaritas and terrific seafood.

"I spent most of my evenings with a twenty-two-year-old beauty named Jane Mason, who came from uppity Tuxedo Park, New York, went to Briarcliff, just about the least inhibited person I'd ever known. She was married to G. Grant Mason, head of Pan American Airways in Cuba, but she didn't let her marriage to stuffy G. Grant get in the way of her adventures with me. We went dancing at the Sans Souci, sometimes with G. Grant in tow, and she often shared my spot at the roulette table in the Nacional. She'd go tooling around Havana with me in her big yellow Packard convertible and often came fishing for days at a time on the *Anita*. I taught her to catch marlin, and she was damn good, as she was pigeon shooting at the Club de Cazadores, the only woman in that male preserve. Sometimes we shot as pairs in big-money bets and we cleaned up. When her husband was away on business, which was often, she came to my room at the Ambos Mundos where I didn't have to be under the coitus interuptus gun. I had never been with a woman as beautiful nor with as unzipped a personality as hers. She was as unpredictable as Zelda Fitzgerald and in some ways like her. Whenever I get black-ass, I cheer up when I think of her standing in the bow of the *Anita* with her strawberry blond hair streaming behind her."

"Did Pauline know about her?" I asked.

"Made sure she did. Unlike hiding my affair with Pauline from Hadley, I wanted Pauline to know what was going on with Jane. I wrote Pauline all about Jane, even sent her a photo of Jane and me on the *Anita*."

"You were giving her plenty of ammunition for a divorce?"

"It was time. But Pauline was not going to make the same mistake as Hadley. No one hundred days. Pauline had staked her claim and she was not going to give in no matter what. Aware of Jane's beauty, she wrote me from the house her uncle Gus had bought for us in Key West, that she was going to have her large nose, imperfect lips, protruding ears, and warts and moles all taken care of before coming to see me in Havana to compete with Jane. When I wrote Pauline that Jane and I had fought a giant marlin for two hours and lost it, she replied that next year she and I would catch enormous ones and when I returned to Key West she would follow me around like a little dog and so would the boys. That's what she actually said: 'like a little dog.' "

"Did you think about starting a divorce?"

"Yes, but I knew she would fight me tooth and nail and the publicity would be bad for the boys. Besides, what grounds would I have? Your Honor, I deserted the family as soon as I could, went off to Wyoming, Key West, Cuba, where I had a great time with a twenty-two-year-old sexy beauty who went overnight fishing with me and tooled around Havana with me and shared my hotel room. So what's my grounds for divorce? My wife, Pauline, made me do it? No, I just had to wait it out, live my life, go on safari without her, spend a little time in Key West, work on planned books like *Death in the Afternoon.*

"As a lure to keep me in Key West, Pauline convinced

her uncle Gus to pony up for a thirty-eight-foot fishing boat that was outfitted especially for me, the *Pilar*, the one we fish on when you visit me in Cuba. Mary and I came here on it. Why don't we go out tomorrow? Gregorio will put out a couple of lines. I don't think marlin are running right now, but there's plenty else."

I said that would be great since I was going back to New York the day after. Gregorio Fuentes was seasoned and skilled in handling the boat when Ernest had a marlin strike, and he took care of *Pilar* while it was berthed in Cojimar, a fishing village near Ernest's finca. I had no doubt Gregorio was the inspiration for the old man in *The Old Man and the Sea*.

"What became of Jane Mason?" I asked.

"Very sad. She had a violent argument with her husband and impetuously jumped, or maybe was pushed, from the second story of their lavish home in Jaimanitas, outside Havana, and broke her back. She had to be carefully transported to New York, where she spent a long time, operations and rehabilitation. When she came back to Cuba a year or so later, we saw each other again, but it wasn't the same."

*Havana Harbor, aboard* Pilar, *with a prized catch in front of Ernest and the beautiful Jane Mason beside him.*

*Chamby, Switzerland, 1922: During their first year in Paris, Ernest and Hadley took a little trip to Chamby.*

# PART TEN

# Paris Is
# Sometimes Sad

E arly the following morning, Gregorio brought *Pilar* to a nearby dock and we headed out to open water for a day of fishing. As usual, when he set foot on the deck, Ernest became uplifted by the sea. Feeling his bare feet on the teak seemed to energize him, and he moved up to the controls and around the boat more solidly than he had around the pool.

It was a treat to be on the breezy, cooling water after the oppressive heat of Key West. We set out arching lines baited for marlin. We also set up additional lines with smaller bait to ensure some good catches even if Ernest's prediction about marlin not running turned out to be true.

It did prove true, but we had compensation. I caught

a good-size wahoo and Ernest had a rough tussle with an eight-foot sailfish that he caught on the marlin line. He brought it in quickly to keep it from being eaten by the sharks, with help from Gregorio's expert maneuvering of the boat.

In the afternoon, Gregorio prepared a wonderful lunch of red grouper, saffron rice, and fried bananas.

After lunch, Ernest went belowdecks for a siesta and I set myself up on the bow, enjoying the streams of flying fish swooping before the boat.

Late that afternoon, Ernest mounted the topside deck and took over the controls from Gregorio, heading the boat back to home base. He took cold beers for us from the wooden icebox that served as his seat. He told me about the time when he and Hadley had the incredible luck of catching sixteen marlins in one string of days, and how that feat meant more to him than netting the Pulitzer Prize.

As twilight faded into dark and the running lights came on, Ernest turned the controls back to Gregorio and we settled aft with daiquiries that Gregorio constructed for us.

"Good old Hotchnick," Ernest said. "Time we get back to Auteuil and make them feel the sting of the Hemhotch Syndicate."

"I'm always ready for Paris," I said.

"So am I, but sometimes it's a little sad. There's the time I stopped on my way back from a safari and Scott happened to be there."

I asked if it was a time he was still with Pauline.

"Yes but not for long. Poor Scott. Terribly black-ass. He'd come to collect some things he'd left in storage."

"Was he with Zelda?"

"No, he had to put her somewhere for safekeeping. He was feeling bereft and sorry for himself, and for her. We were having dinner at the Closerie. 'Just imagine,' he said, 'ten years ago we were the Golden Girl and her Debonair Husband, the genius writer. And now look at us. She's put away and I'm a relic. You remember I used to say I wanted to die at thirty—well, I'm past thirty and the end's near. I used to have two pleasures—writing and getting a little tight. When things were bad with Zelda and I was down, I could always go to the Ritz bar where I'd get back my self-esteem for half an hour. But then, having to take Zelda to those sanitariums, I had to get seriously drunk before I could leave her, and the next day I'd pay the usual penalties for my drunkenness. I tried to write, but I'd forgot how I had dragged *Gatsby* out of the pit of my stomach in a time of misery. Now I have the misery, but the pit of my stomach is full of Beaujolais. So, you see, the pleasure of work and the pleasure of drink are both gone, and I have lost Zelda for God knows how long, and I am over thirty. So it's fitting and proper for me to die. You were right, Hem, when you said a rummy married to a crazy is not a winning combination.'

"I told him he was also right about me. During those awful one hundred days he had called the shot: A man, torn between two women, will lose both of them. I told him that Pauline was finally divorcing me."

" 'Oh Christ, we're some pair of losers, aren't we?' "

"I made a mistake with Pauline, that's all. A goddamn fatal mistake. The troops retreated when they should have advanced. No matter what they tell you about re-living the past, it's not a bridge, and you can't go back over it. Maybe if I hadn't been so successful so fast . . . don't really know. Those years away from Paris, married to Pauline, I lost my sense of what counted, and what didn't. Her wealth and my easy fame made living a snap. We had separate lives. Nothing shared. Not even the boys. Pauline always had plenty of help looking after them. Her money corrupted both of us. She couldn't decide who she was or who she wanted to be. She wanted some of me to rub off on her. She pursued; I avoided.

"It wasn't any one thing. We didn't quarrel. Actually, we were very considerate of each other, but as a couple, we'd gone flat. Being together was boring. Weren't connected. Nothing much to talk about. Mostly did things apart. Each had our own group of friends and they didn't mesh. She tried to use her wealth to connect us, but it just put me off. I'd made it on my own and I had to keep it that way.

" 'I warned you about fame,' Scott said; 'struggle is a hell of a lot better.'

"Gave Scott my lucky piece," Ernest said, "my well-worn rabbit's foot to give to Zelda."

" 'But what'll you have?' he asked.

" 'Don't need it anymore, I told him, had all the good luck I can handle."

Gregorio brought us some fried octopus and re-freshed our daiquiris.

"You must have been relieved," I said, "finally getting your divorce from Pauline."

"Pretty much, but it had its sad downside. After my shaky beginning with the boys—I told you about taking off when they were babies; I'm just no good at those first couple of diaper and colic years—but afterward I tried to make up for it. With Bumby, everything was fine between us. We had regular visits and he spent vacations with me. In the war he rose to the rank of captain with the OSS—his grown-up name was Jack. He parachuted behind the German lines, eventually captured, but escaped and had a good war record and I thought he'd make the military his career but he opted out and became a bond salesman.

"With Gregory and Patrick, it was all right until the divorce. Gigi [Gregory's nickname] was the one I was closest to. When we played baseball in the clearing in front of the finca, Gigi used to try to knock everybody's cap off on the first pitch to get you off the plate. He did it to me, too, and I walked out to him, having picked myself up from the dirt, and said, 'Don't you know any better than to throw at your own father?' Looking at me as mean as a warthog, he said, 'Don't you know there aren't any fathers on a ball field?'

"He was a very polite boy when not competing, the only one of the three that I declared to win with. But he had this miserable lace-curtain Catholic education at Canterbury School where he hated the masters and did not like the boys, and it inhibited the hell out of him. I have a Cheyenne great-great-grandmother and Gig was the only boy that turned out Indian, not Cherokee, Digger, Paiute, Navajo, or any of those unfortunate people, but Northern Cheyenne, and he has all the problems of them, as I always had.

"It all changed between Gig and Patrick and me when Pauline got her divorce and she deliberately started to turn both boys against me and made a hell of a conflict in them when there wasn't any. As a result, Gig's life blew up. He'd gone to medical school, but after the divorce and Pauline's rampage against me, he got into heavy drinking and drugs and deviant behavior. I won't go into all of it, but what was very upsetting was his run-in with the law. Pauline was in charge of him and I tried to get her to take command, but Gig was too far gone and beyond my being able to do anything for him."

Ernest said that he got along all right with Patrick although they never became close due to the terrible time when Patrick came to visit Ernest in Cuba. The day after he arrived, Ernest said, Patrick had an attack that was caused by a concussion he had suffered the day before in Key West, when an MG his brother was driving with Patrick in the passenger seat, ran into a tree. Ernest said that for weeks Patrick's mind was garbled and he struggled physically. Ernest said he stayed at Patrick's side night and day all through the attack, got him good doctors and special help, but when he recovered and his mind cleared, Patrick had no memory of what had happened, and that's when Pauline told him that Ernest had abandoned and neglected him, and that everything Ernest had done in Cuba, she transferred to having been done by her in Key West. "So, no wonder he was put off by me," Ernest said, "but he was a good kid. He made magna cum laude at Harvard, and then went on to Tanganyika, where he became a white hunter and did successful experiments in raising corn there."

"You're right, Papa," I said, "that's sad about the boys."

"Something even sadder happened that time in Paris." He slowly shook his head and took his time remembering.

"I was at Lipp's on their enclosed terrace having a drink—there was a taxi stand there and a cab pulled up to discharge a passenger and damn if it wasn't Hadley. Hadn't laid eyes on her since our divorce. She was very well dressed and as beautiful as I remembered her. As I approached her, she saw me, gasped, and threw her arms around me. Having her up against me shortened my breath. She stepped back and looked at me.

" 'My goodness, Ernest,' she said, 'you look the same.'

" 'Not you.'

" 'Oh?'

" 'You look even lovelier.'

" 'I follow you in the newspapers. *A Farewell to Arms* was wonderful. You're a romantic, you know.'

" 'Are you still living here?'

" 'Yes, for a while.'

" 'You still married to what's his name?'

" 'Yes, I'm still Mrs. What's His Name.'

"I invited her into Lipp's for champagne. We discussed people we knew and what had become of them. I said, 'You know, Hadley, I think about you often.'

" 'Even now?'

" 'You know what I'm remembering—that evening when *The Sun Also Rises* was published, and I put on my one necktie and we went to the Ritz and drank champagne with *fraises des bois* in the bottom of the glass. There's something romantic about poverty when you're young and hopeful.'

" 'I remember,' she said, 'and I also remember the time you sprained your ankle and we had to get you down the mountain with you sitting on your skis.'

" 'You and I learned to ski at the same time, but you were far better than I was.'

" 'Not better, just a bit more cautious, and besides, you had a leg full of shrapnel. It's a wonder you could ski at all. Did you know I never skied again after we parted?'

" 'And I never went back to Schruns or Bludenz or any of those other places that were ours. Those picnics on the infield at the Enghien races and the first time we discovered Pamplona and Cortina d'Ampezzo, the Black Forest, and the songs we used to sing.' I started to sing and Hadley picked up on it:

*A feather kitty's talent lies*
*In scratching out the other's eyes.*
*A feather kitty never dies*
*Oh immortality.*

" 'You know, Hadley, just yesterday I saw a Gypsy begging for coins and I recalled what a beautiful Gypsy you were that time in the Camargue.'

" 'Oh, my goodness, you remembered that? The way we stained ourselves with walnut juice so we could crash that Gypsy dance?'

" 'Yeah, all excited, thinking about the food and the flowing wine.'

" 'We must have been very hungry to crash a Gypsy dance.'

" 'We were starving. We ran out of money, don't you remember? We hadn't eaten for a couple of days.'

" 'And then we found out—there wasn't anything to eat, no wine, just Gypsies dancing in the dust.'

" 'The worst part was that it took over a week for the walnut stain to wear off.'

" 'You made a very handsome Gypsy—I can still see you with that silk scarf tied around your forehead.'

"I asked if she could have dinner with me. She looked at me, remembering me. She gave it some thought.

" 'I guess not,' " I said, " 'I have no sinister motive— just to look at you across a table for a little while.'

" 'You know, Ernest,' she said, 'if things hadn't been so good between us, I might not have left you so quickly.'

" 'How many times I thought I saw you passing by. Once in a taxi stopped at a light. Another time in the

Louvre I followed a woman that had the color of your hair and the way you walk and the set of your shoulders. I followed her all through the museum. You would think that with the passage of time, not being with you or hearing from you, you would fade away, but no, you are as much with me now as you were then.'

" 'And I'll always love you, Tatie. As I loved you in Oak Park and as I loved you here in Paris.' She raised her glass and touched it with mine. She drank the last of her champagne and put down her glass. 'I must go to my appointment,' she said.

"I accompanied her to the corner and waited with her for the light to change. I said I remembered those dreams we dreamed with nothing on our table and the wine bottle empty. 'But you believed in me against those tough odds. I want you to know, Hadley, you'll be the true part of any woman I write about. I'll spend the rest of my life looking for you.'

" 'Good-bye, my Tatie.'

"The light changed to green. Hadley turned and kissed me, a meaningful kiss; then she crossed the street and I watched her go, that familiar, graceful walk."


The shore lights began to appear in the distance and faraway music skimmed along the water. Ernest leaned his head back and closed his eyes, perhaps seeing Hadley departing from Lipp's, turning her head to take a last look at him before disappearing into the crowded sidewalk.

As Gregorio steered toward the approaching dock, Ernest said, "That was the last time I saw her."

*Finca Vigía, 1960: The last picture I took of Ernest before his precipitous departure from Cuba, where he left all his possessions, never to return.*

*Ernest at his home in Ketchum, Idaho, after his first, unexpected release from the psychiatric section of St. Mary's Hospital. He had to be forcefully readmitted not long after I took this picture.*

# PART ELEVEN

# That Room at
# St. Mary's

Señor Pecas," Ernest said as he and nurse Susan returned to the room, a big smile on his face on seeing me sitting at the window. "How about some tea for El Pecas and me, Susie," he said to the nurse.

"It's time for your nap, Mr. Hemingway," she said.

"And it's time I get out of here, but let's start with the tea and then the nap, which is a word that belongs in the nursery, and so do you."

Nurse Susan left for the tea.

"You use the one chair, Pecas. I'll get on the bed. You should have seen those two doctors taking my fluctuating blood pressure over and over, trying to decide how many more ECTs I could tolerate. 'You've already wrecked most of my memory,' I told them, 'so keep zapping me so I can forget the two of you.' "

"Are they going to stop?"

"What those shock doctors don't know," Ernest said, "is about writers and such things as remorse and contrition and what they do to them. They should make all psychiatrists take a course in creative writing so they'd know about writers. Let's change the subject. You see Coop before you left Hollywood?"

"Yes, at his house." Ernest was referring to movie star Gary Cooper, who had been a good friend of his from way back when Coop played Lieutenant Henry in the early film version of *A Farewell to Arms.* Cooper had also starred in *For Whom the Bell Tolls,* which had been a box-office success but not with Ernest who thought the co-star, Ingrid Bergman, instead of looking like the peasant woman of the book, looked like she sprang from Helena Rubinstein out of Abercrombie and Fitch. And Ernest was annoyed that Coop had sex with Ingrid in the famous sleeping bag scene with his jacket buttoned up. Nevertheless, Coop was set to star in a film Ernest and I planned to make of *Across the River and into the Trees,* but it had been called off now because of Coop's tragic discovery that he had terminal prostate cancer. When I went to visit him, he was a wasted figure lying immobile in his darkened bedroom.

"I phoned Coop couple days ago," Ernest said. "He's pretty far down the road, isn't he? He bet me that he'd beat me to the barn. That's cojones for you! Forget all the fancy crap—dignity, courage, fortitude—bullshit! All you need to die right, cojones!"

I knew that Ernest had always had strong feelings about dying, especially now, and that being accused of courting death had elicited a strong response from him.

"It has been emphasized that I have sought death all my life. If you have spent your life avoiding death as cagily as possible, but on the other hand taking no backchat from her and studying her as you would a beautiful harlot who could put you soundly to sleep forever with no problems and no necessity to work, you could be said to have studied her, but you have not sought her. Because you know among one or two other things that if you sought her, you would possess her, and from her reputation you know that she would present you with an incurable disease. So much for the constant pursuit of death. She's just another whore."

Nurse Susan returned with a tray bearing two tea mugs and two cookies. Ernest said he had stashed a bottle of vodka for the tea, but she found it. Susie the snooper. She smiled at him and left.

We sipped our tea and munched our cookies.

I told Ernest how moved I was reading his loving tribute to Hadley in the final chapter he had given me. I said, "No man has ever loved a woman more or written about that love so tenderly. I only wish that one day I would meet a woman I would love like that."

"Hadley and I were lucky. The stars were perfectly aligned for us. Hadley believed in me and that was more than enough to overcome the pain of all the rejection slips. Those stories—it was hard as hell to write 'em but harder to have them rejected. When you get a printed form attached to a story you wrote and worked on very hard and believed in, the printed rejection slip is hard to take on an empty stomach. Dear Sir, we regret to tell you that your submission does not meet our editorial needs. Well fuck 'em! I regret to tell you that your rejection slip does not meet *my* editorial needs!

"Hadley would notice the mutilated rejection slips and tell me not to be discouraged, that she loved my stories and that someday somebody would publish them and they would be a big success and my picture would be in bookstore windows, smiling and holding a pipe.

"She would put her hands on the sides of my face and pull me toward her and hold me and make me feel we had something no one else had and that it would carry us wherever we wanted to go."

"That certainly comes across in your lovely book," I said. "Who was the pilot fish who led the rich to you?"

"John Dos Passos. He meant well but should have known better."

"And the rich?"

"Sara and Gerald Murphy."

"But they were devoted to you."

"Too much."

"But the Paris you wrote about served you very well."

"The best of that I wrote long ago. If only I could finish it. Just one true sentence to cap it off. I stand here at this table trying one day after another, but nothing comes. Those goddamn doctors with their blasts to my brain, the fucking torture of it, they've wiped me out, nothing to call up, no reserves."

"They're trying to keep you from killing yourself."

"But what have they given me to keep me going? I'm sixty-one years old and I'm empty. The books and stories I promised myself to write will never be written. What does a man of my age care about? Being healthy. Working good at his calling. Eating and drinking with the people he cares about. Good sex, traveling to the places he loves. I'm denied all of 'em. Why should I stick around? How do I pay the goddamn taxes if I can't write the stuff that pays for them? They're after me, I tell you.

The hall phone's bugged and so is this room. Nurse Susan feeds reports to the FBI."

"Papa, you've got to get over this craziness."

"Crazy, am I? Well, just be careful what you say when she's in the room."

"Why would the FBI . . ."

"I write suspicious books that take place in foreign countries: France and Italy, Communist Cuba and fascist Spain. I lived among the Cuban Communists all those years. I shoot guns. I speak languages J. Edgar Hoover doesn't understand. My lawyer, my doctor, my banker, all of them in cahoots with him. They've stripped my bank account. I probably can't pay my hospital bill. They're after me for back taxes. I've tried to live the right way, but they only want it their way, so I'm giving my life back to them. They can take my life and stick it. Here is my life with a bullet in it. That's what they want? Take it! It's all yours!"

The phobias, delusions, fears, obsessions hadn't changed. The words were the very words I had heard again and again.

"Ernest, listen, we need you here; a world of people need you here."

"Too late, Pecas. I've got my exit visa."

Tears were in his eyes now. It had grown dark and the streetlamps outside the window were reflecting into the room. Ernest bent his head against his chest and closed his eyes. Hospital sounds were coming from the corridor. The siren of an ambulance entering the hospital grounds cut into the room, its whirling red light flashing the window as it passed by. There were muffled announcements summoning doctors. I felt very close to Ernest. He was indeed Papa. He was in pain, but the doctors were not relieving it. Not capable. Nor was I.

Ernest raised his head and nodded a few times, as if acknowledging some inner thought or yearning or admission.

"Pecas," he said in a soft, barely audible voice, "tell me this: How does a young man know when he falls in love for the very first time, how can he know that it will be the only true love of his life? How can he possibly know? How can he know?"

He looked at me intently, as if searching for an answer.

He took off his glasses, placed them on the bedside table, and wiped his eyes with the top edge of the sheet, leaving the sheet covering his face. From under the sheet, he repeated, "How can he possibly know?"

The room was dead quiet. There were faraway street sounds. "Pecas," Ernest said from his foxhole, "I guess I better take a little snooze or nurse Susie will snitch on me. With any luck . . . maybe I'll dream of Paris."

I sat there for a spell. It was time for me to go. I had a plane to catch, but I felt disloyal leaving him in this caged room; this fine man who had given so much of himself, to wind up with so little. I was grieving for him and the scant life that was being parceled out to him in this unjust endgame.

This man, who had stood his ground against charging water buffalo, who had flown bombing missions over Germany, who had refused to accept the prevailing style of writing but, enduring poverty and rejection, had insisted on writing in his own unique way, this man, my deepest friend, was now afraid—afraid that the FBI was after him, that his body was disintegrating, that his friends had turned on him, that living was no longer an option.

Most of all, I grieved at my helplessness to rescue him from this raging storm.

He was asleep now. I sat there remembering what he had once said about dreaming:

"When I dream of afterlife in heaven, the action always takes place in the Paris Ritz. It's a fine summer night. I knock back a couple of martinis at the bar, Cambon side. Then there's a wonderful dinner under a flowering chestnut tree in Le Petit Jardin, the little garden that faces the Grill. After a few brandies, I wander up to my room and slip into one of those huge Ritz beds. They are all made of brass. There's a bolster for my head the size of the Graf Zeppelin and four square pillows filled with real goose feathers—two for me, and two for my quite heavenly companion."

If I stayed another day, two days, more, I could not bring him respite, only aggravate my own despair. Reluctantly, I stood up and crossed the room, the stab of his thin, seeking voice forever in my ear: "How can he know that it will be the only true love of his life? How can he know?"

I opened the door. The corridor was empty.

I quietly let the door close to its latch, hoping my friend was dreaming of being in his favorite room at the Ritz, on the garden side, in a huge brass bed with a heavenly companion who, I'm sure, is Hadley.

*Ernest outside his Ketchum home, as I remember him.*

# Postscript

Two weeks after I left him, without completing the pre-scribed cycle of ECTs, the Mayo doctors released Ernest from the hospital.

One week after that, in his house in Ketchum, Idaho, he took his life.

Fifty years after his death, in response to a Freedom of Information petition, the FBI released its Hemingway file. It revealed that beginning in the 1940s J. Edgar Hoover had placed Ernest under surveillance because he was suspicious of Ernest's activities in Cuba. Over the follow-ing years, agents filed reports on him and tapped his phones. The surveillance continued all through his confinement at St. Mary's Hospital. It is likely that the phone in the hall outside his room was tapped and that nurse Susan may well have been an FBI informant.

Ernest's tribute to Paris and Hadley was published after his death. I honored him by giving the book its title: *A Moveable Feast*.

My wish that one day I would meet a woman I would love like he loved Hadley came true.

# Photograph Credits

Photo of Ernest and Hotchner at El Choko bar during La Feria de San Fermín. Pamplona, Spain, 1954. A. E. Hotchner's personal collection.

Photo of Ernest and his wife, Mary, huddled over his presents at his sixtieth birthday party. Churriana, Spain, 1959. A. E. Hotchner.

Photo of wreckage of the first of Ernest's two consecutive plane crashes. Uganda, Africa, 1954. Courtesy of the Ernest Hemingway Collection at the John F. Kennedy Presidential Library and Museum, Boston.

Photo of Ernest suffereing multiple injuries after the second consecutive rescue plane crashed in Africa in 1954. Courtesy of the Ernest Hemingway Collection at the John F. Kennedy Presidential Library and Museum, Boston.

Photo (from left) of Gerald Murphy, Sara Murphy, Pauline Pfeiffer, Ernest, and Hadley Hemingway sharing a table at the *feria*. Pamplona, Spain, 1926. Courtesy of the Ernest Hemingway Collection at the John F. Kennedy Presidential Library and Museum, Boston.

Photo of Ernest with little Bumby and Hadley during a happy respite from Paris's brutal winter. Schruns, Austria, 1925. A. E. Hotchner's personal collection.

Photo of Ernest at our picnic at the Irati River when a gentle hound mysteriously appeared out of the adjoining forest. Pamplona, Spain, 1959. A. E. Hotchner.

Photo of Ernest with his buddy, Joe "Sloppy" Russell, in 1932 when they went to Havana to get away from the Key West house for an extended period and fish for marlin. Courtesy of the Ernest Hemingway Collection at the John F. Kennedy Presidential Library and Museum, Boston.

Photo of Ernest in his saltwater pool in Key West, where I took his picture when I visited him there in 1955. A. E. Hotchner.

Photo of Ernest and Hadley's wedding day, attended by Ernest's sister, Ursula, his mother, and his little brother, Leicester. Horton Bay, Michigan, September 3, 1921. Courtesy of the Ernest Hemingway Collection at the John F. Kennedy Presidential Library and Museum, Boston.

Photo of Ernest on the beach with Pauline in 1927. Courtesy of the Ernest Hemingway Collection at the John F. Kennedy Presidential Library and Museum, Boston.

Photo of the all-male safari that deliberately excluded Pauline: Ben Fourie, Charles Thompson, Philip Percival, and Ernest with their kudu and oryx antlers. Kujungu Camp, Tanganyika, Africa, 1934. Courtesy of the Ernest Hemingway Collection at the John F. Kennedy Presidential Library and Museum, Boston.

Photo of Pauline, who sometimes trimmed Ernest's hair during his periodic returns to Key West. Courtesy of the Ernest Hemingway Collection at the

John F. Kennedy Presidential Library and Museum, Boston.

Photo of Ernest with a prized catch and the beautiful Jane Mason beside him, aboard the *Pilar* in Havana Harbor. Courtesy of the Ernest Hemingway Collection at the John F. Kennedy Presidential Library and Museum, Boston.

Photo of Ernest and Hadley during their first year in Paris when they took a little trip to Chamby, Switzerland, in 1922. Courtesy of the Ernest Hemingway Collection at the John F. Kennedy Presidential Library and Museum, Boston.

Photo of Ernest, the last one I took before his precipitous departure from Cuba, where he left all his possessions, never to return. Finca Vigia, 1960. A. E. Hotchner.

Photo of Ernest at his home in Ketchum, Idaho, after his first, unexpected release from the psychiatric section of St. Mary's Hospital. He had to be forcefully readmitted not long after I took this picture. A. E. Hotchner.

Photo of Ernest outside his Ketchum home, as I remember him. A. E. Hotchner.

...see you. It is a real new...
...bout cut the sugar...
the old days you would...
Hope those g...
Enclose the check for...
I...we are go...
Shelter house off...
cleaves (mine)

Need very best...
of my Saint's Day...
Sa...